Between Dog and Wolf

Understanding the Connection and the Confusion

Jessica Addams
and Andrew Miller

Wenatchee, WA

Between Dog and Wolf
Understanding the Connection and the Confusion
Jessica Addams and Andrew Miller

Dogwise Publishing
A Division of Direct Book Service, Inc.
403 South Mission Street, Wenatchee, Washington 98801
509-663-9115, 1-800-776-2665
www.dogwisepublishing.com / info@dogwisepublishing.com

© 2012 Jessica Addams and Andrew Miller

Graphic design: Lindsay Peternell
Cover photo: Monty Sloan. Abe (left) is a northern mix *dog*. Maggie (right) is a *wolf*. They are play-chasing in a fenced yard at an animal sanctuary called *Mission: Wolf* in Gardner, Colorado.
Interior photographs and illustrations: Jessica Addams, Julia Ballarin, David Brezinski, Kevin Cole, Sara Goldsmith, Ethan Hall, C J Hughson, Lindy Ireland, Marek Kultys, Monty Sloan, Ryan Talbot and Karoliina Toivanen.

All rights reserved. No part of this book may be reproduced or transmitted in any form or by any means, electronic, digital or mechanical, including photocopying, recording or by any information storage or retrieval system without permission in writing from the publisher.

Limits of Liability and Disclaimer of Warranty:
The authors and publisher shall not be liable in the event of incidental or consequential damages in connection with, or arising out of, the furnishing, performance, or use of the instructions and suggestions contained in this book.

Library of Congress Cataloging-in-Publication Data
Addams, Jessica, 1976-
  Between dog and wolf : understanding the connection and the confusion / Jessica Addams, Andrew Miller.
     p. cm.
  Includes index.

  1. Dogs--Behavior. 2. Dogs--Psychology. 3. Wolves--Behavior. 4. Wolves--Psychology. 5. Comparison (Psychology) I. Miller, Andrew, 1981- II. Title.
SF433.A33 2012
636.7--dc23
                              2011047181

Printed in the U.S.A.

This book is dedicated to all the friends,
two-legged and four-legged, who have
accompanied us on our journeys.

Table of Contents

Acknowledgements vii
A Note from the Authors ix
Foreword xi
Introduction 1

1. Modern Wolf Mythology 5
2. So What are Wolves and Dogs Really Like? 20
3. Domestication: From Wolf to Dog 50
4. When Wolves and Dogs Combine: A Genetics Primer 63
5. Variable Outcomes: It's Not That Simple 72
6. Practical Advice for Rescue Organizations and Shelters 99
7. The Current State of DNA Testing 140
8. Conclusions 150

Appendix A—A Brief Mention of Another Suspicious Species 154
Appendix B—Facility Contact Information 158

Recommended Reading 161
Bibliography 163
About the Authors 176
Index 178

Acknowledgments

Profound and grateful thanks are due to the following colleagues for editing, encouragement, and hysterical screaming.

> Ray Coppinger
> Pat Goodmann
> Monty Sloan

All of our review readers, especially Deb Biesemeier and Nicole Wilde.

And the staff of every animal facility we have visited, both in our lives at Wolf Park and during our direct research for this book. Your hospitality and generosity were unparalleled, and your assistance has been invaluable.

In addition, we would like to thank our parents—without whom this would have been considerably more difficult—and all the many animals who have touched our lives.

Note from the Authors

While we had several goals in writing this book, what led us down this path initially was our interest in helping people identify wolf hybrids, which got its start during our tenure at Wolf Park. People would bring in all sorts of animals wondering if they had a wolf, a dog or something in between. Often there were dire consequences riding on making a proper identification. People who have worked with these animals for a long time and who have developed expertise with their behaviors and handling can usually tell a wolf from a dog, especially if they can meet the animal in person. Most casual observers, however, cannot. Since not all people can quickly or conveniently get their animals to an expert for identification, we were inspired to create a "manual" of sorts for people to use when expert opinions are not readily available.

We wish to emphasize that this volume is a *practical* approach to wolves, dogs, and hybrids. It is designed for use by people who do not have, and/or cannot easily obtain, much experience working with a variety of such animals in a range of situations and environments. No matter how much experience or knowledge an individual has, no human can determine the actual genetic percentage of wolf in an animal just through observation. At best, one can get an indication of how close to a "wolf" or "dog" *standard* the animal *appears* to be on the basis of looks and behavior. While neither we nor anyone else can reach irrefutable conclusions about an animal's genetics, our analysis is still of practical use in everyday situations and in handling the animal. So, while a dedicated team of experienced scientists with access to a vast array of expensive testing apparatus and highly technical knowledge can, in some instances, determine the genetic makeup of an individual animal to some degree given enough time, this is rarely of use to people in immediate situations in daily life. In this book, along with many other issues of interest, we explore the options available to those who only rarely encounter wolves and hybrids, and who may need to make a decision on an animal's identity with accuracy and speed knowing that its life may depend on their conclusions. Scientists are working on new methods of analysis, but they are as yet unavailable to or inconvenient for use by the general populace.

Concerning terminology

We are about to enter a sea of sloppy language. In this book, we spend many pages explaining how the terms "wolf" and "dog" are apparently arbitrary markings along a continuum of varying physiology and behavior, and how a member of one species can and will sometimes look and behave just like a member of the other. However, it becomes unwieldy trying to refer to "animals which look and act mostly like pure, wild type wolves are expected to look and act" and "animals which look and act mostly like purebred dogs are expected to look and act." As we go along, if things get confusing, please consider the word "wolves" to mean "wolves, or any canids which exhibit primarily *wolf* behavior—behavior which is commonly expected of a wild animal" and the word "dogs" to mean "dogs, or any canids which exhibit primarily *dog* behavior—behavior which is commonly expected of a domesticated pet."

Further complicating all of this is that, around the world, wolves display a huge range of physiological and behavioral attributes. Not all wolves closely resemble the gray wolf (*Canis lupus*) which is the most commonly seen wolf in the United States—either behaviorally or physiologically. Since our primary experience is with, and the focus of this book is on, the offspring of gray wolves and domestic dogs in the United States, our statements about wolves in general will refer primarily to these North American gray wolves. For those interested in different sub-species of wolves in other parts of the world, all we can say is, "your mileage may vary."

In the same vein, use of the phrase "wolf hybrid" to refer to animals which have both wolf and dog ancestry is not entirely accurate. A "hybrid" is formally defined by the *Compact Oxford English Dictionary* as "the offspring of two plants or animals of different species or varieties," but as our knowledge of wolves and dogs has grown, we have found them to be so closely related as to be considered members of the same species. Therefore, technically, an animal with both wolf and dog ancestry is not a hybrid, or crossing of two different species, but rather simply an admixture of individuals expressing two extremes within one species. Thus, a more correct term is "wolfdog." However, since the most commonly used term for these animals (coined when scientists still thought wolves and dogs were different species) is "wolf hybrid," we use it here to avoid (further) confusion.

We have included an extensive bibliography at the end of the book and provide citations throughout to give credit to the research upon which much of our work is built. This is the literature we recommend that the reader explore if more information on this fascinating subject is desired.

One more brief note: Since there are two authors at work here, we refer to ourselves as "we" and "us" where applicable.

Foreword (and Barkward)

By Monty Sloan

We humans have a very special relationship with dogs that is different from that which we have with any other animal. It is a deep seated love/hate relationship, involving extreme love and extreme cruelty. But this relationship goes much further than the relatively recent "pet" phenomenon that has only blossomed over the past century or so. It goes much further back, possibly very far back in early human development. A question has arisen: has our relationship with dogs, which are now generally accepted as having been directly descended from wolves, also led to the development of human culture? If so, we owe a lot to dogs and their wolf ancestors—yet many dogs are treated very poorly by man and, as for wolves, well, overall they are still vilified and many populations have been driven to extinction!

This book is a wonderful look into our perceptions of wolves and dogs and how the media influences our ideas about animals. In a very entertaining way, the book delves into the human thought process, how we learn, and how we come to conclusions. As Barry Lopez detailed the history of human attitudes towards wolves in *Of Wolves and Men*, this book investigates the human learning process and how that leads to what we think we know.

When you look at what most people know, or think they know, about canines (both our domestic companions and their cousins in the wild), it becomes apparent that there is a basic lack of knowledge and understanding. Many common sources of information are full of confusion—even misinformation. From all varieties of sources there may be "quality control" problems. Anything—from the Internet, to books, to TV, to our friends, and even professionals—our sources of information can be biased, incorrect, or completely wrong. Nobody can know everything, even collectively. Science is still pursuing the intricate details about the biology and behavior of dogs.

Pet owners, caretakers, veterinarians, trainers, and yes, biologists and behaviorists, too, all have their own individual knowledge base and their own opinions. This is especially true when it comes to the subject of dogs, as they are so closely familiar. Consider the lack of understanding most have of canine behavior, communication, ecology, physiology, and ethnology. What do we "know" about that neighbor's "scary" wolf hybrid, or the incessantly barking dog down the street, or the dog sleeping on our bed? Then go further and try to extrapolate what you think you know about dogs and how that pertains to what you think you know about wolves—all the knowledge you have based on a myriad of sources, some factual, some not—and it is no wonder that man's best friend, and his closest relative, the wolf, find a cautionary relationship with humans. One has to ponder that perhaps the dog is man's best friend only because the dog is so forgiving.

Wolf or dog? Photo courtesy of Monty Sloan.

Books on dogs have become commonplace. New books are being published so often it is nearly impossible to keep up. Books on wolves, though less common, are still frequent enough in publication that only the most devout wolf fan can keep up with them all. But when it comes to any publications on a surprisingly commonplace, yet controversial, animal—the wolf-dog hybrid, not to mention the pet wolf—the number of worthwhile books is so small that a child could easily hold all of them in one hand. With the publication of this book, the child would need to be a bit stronger.

Along with sound information about wolves, dogs and wolf-dog hybrids, this book helps the reader understand how we as humans learn and how we know what we know, or don't know, and how to simply keep an open mind! There is truth everywhere, but finding it through all the clutter is the key, and misunderstanding is the enemy. This can be said of any aspect of life. Perhaps this book will help correct some misunderstandings and shed a little light on our canine friends.

Monty Sloan, wolf photographer and behaviorist
Wolf Park, Battle Ground, Indiana
www.wolfphotography.com

Introduction

We cut our behavioral teeth, so to speak, at Wolf Park, in Battle Ground, Indiana. The Park is an education and research facility which has been working with socialized (hand-raised) gray wolves since 1972. During the our tenure there, the Park received many calls each month from humane societies, rescues, and laypeople who had in their possession an animal which had somehow gotten the label "wolf hybrid." Whether the animals actually merited that label was anyone's guess. Some animals had been surrendered to rescues, with the surrendering individual giving the animal's breed as "wolf hybrid." Some had been found wandering the streets and just "looked wolfy." A few concerned dog owners had been told by strangers, neighbors, or even their own veterinarians that their animal "looked like a wolf." These animals were generally in danger of being euthanized, either because the local shelter considered all wolf hybrids unadoptable by default and/or no rescue facility could be found. Even if the animal's owner had experienced years of perfect behavior from an animal suddenly revealed to be a wolf hybrid (rightly or wrongly), he or she would likely feel unprepared to deal with an animal which was now presumed to be at least part wolf.

Many of these concerned individuals sent photos or video of the animals involved, often in hopes of getting a second opinion. While it is not currently possible to determine an exact amount of wolf content via a DNA test or otherwise (see our explanation later in this book), it is possible, through viewing of photographs and/or behavioral descriptions (and, of course, through viewing the animal in person), to make an educated guess about how many "wolfy" characteristics a given animal displays, and thereby its probable suitability as a pet. Sometimes, this educated guess isn't even necessary. The photos the Park received revealed that most of the animals in question—perhaps seventy percent—were mostly, or even all, dog. Some were blatantly dogs: forty pound, blue eyed, curly tailed, purebred Siberian Huskies. Others were more difficult to pin down. Some of the animals were definitely wolves or high-content hybrids, but most were "dog-oids"—canine animals of mixed ancestry which physically resembled wolves in some ways, but resembled dogs behaviorally and would likely make perfectly adequate pets if given the chance.

A handsome pair of "dog-oids," canids of indefinite ancestry, residents of a wolf hybrid rescue facility. Photo courtesy of Ryan Talbot.

Czechoslovakian Wolf-Dog—all dog, but you might not know it just by looking. Photo courtesy of Monty Sloan.

INTRODUCTION

It distressed us that many of these animals—essentially dogs—were unnecessarily euthanized or surrendered to a rescue, simply because someone had felt the need to stamp them with the label "wolf hybrid." The label spelled certain death for many individual animals, since many owners or rescuers did not wish to deal with something they had heard described as wild and potentially dangerous. They felt they needed to place or otherwise dispose of the animal as quickly as possible. We saw several perfectly good dogs lose their homes after their owners were casually told the animal "looked like a wolf." The owner would go home, look up "wolf hybrid" on the Internet, panic, and immediately try to get rid of the animal. We saw people who had rescued feral animals off the streets trying desperately to find a facility which would not immediately euthanize a "wolfy-looking" animal. We even saw a retired police officer forced to euthanize his perfectly well-behaved "Czechoslovakian wolf dog," a breed of dog which has wolves in its distant past, but whose current members are essentially all dog—solely because his landlord believed it was a wolf.

The original goal of this book was to convince those who hold the lives of these animals in their hands to give them a second chance, and to better prepare individuals who may be faced with this decision. We hoped to provide a resource for people who had found an unusual canine on the street, had been given a "wolf hybrid" puppy by a friend or relative, or who worked at a veterinary office or animal shelter and had someone bring in an animal of unknown heritage and suspicious behavior with its breed given as "wolf hybrid." Our desire was to provide an armament of background information which would help people who do not normally work with wolves to evaluate unknown canines on the basis of knowledge and not just on an arbitrary estimate of "wolf percentage." This would give them the ability to make an informed decision about what kind of pet the animal would likely make. We wished to help readers to cast aside some of the mythology surrounding wolf hybrids and to look at each individual animal as the potentially adoptable companion it might become.

We would like to think that we have accomplished this original goal, but as we had more people review the manuscript and got input from our publishers, we realized that the broader subject of what makes a wolf a wolf and what makes a dog a dog is not only relevant to those interested in wolf hybrids, but would appeal to a more general audience as well. Thus, helping people understand the difference and similarities between wolves and dogs became another goal of ours in writing this book. There seems to be an increasing interest in comparing and contrasting wolves and dogs, since studies in recent years have shown that dogs evolved from wolves in the not-too-distant past. And, due to a number of factors which we will discuss in the book, there has been a trend among some authors and television personalities to try to take what they *think they know* about wolves and their behavior and apply it to dogs. It's true that wolves and dogs can look a lot alike and in some ways appear to act alike. But just because a dog has some superficial characteristics that someone considers "wolfy" does not mean it should be treated like a wolf.

"Those of us who lack the opportunity of forming our own opinions on any particular subject are apt to accept the opinions of others... The author who first used the words 'as cruel as a tiger' and 'as bloodthirsty as a tiger' when attempting to emphasize the evil character of the villain of his piece, not only showed a lamentable ignorance of the animal he defamed, but coined phrases which have come into universal circulation, and which are mainly responsible for the wrong opinion of the tigers held by all except that very small proportion of the public who have the opportunity of forming their own opinions."

~ Jim Corbett, turn-of-the-century hunter of man-eating big cats

"To know that we know what we know, and that we do not know what we do not know, that is true knowledge."

~ Henry David Thoreau

A wolf as one might encounter in the wild. Photo courtesy of Monty Sloan.

Chapter 1
Modern Wolf Mythology: The Things That "Everyone Knows"

All trees have bark.
All dogs bark.
Therefore, all dogs are trees.
~Unknown

Everyone knows what a dog is.

Dogs are featured in our favorite television shows and movies. Our neighbors have dogs. Our friends have dogs. Our families have dogs. Dogs appear on postcards, in glossy magazines, and in books. They walk down the street each day, accompanied by their adoring owners. Our police and armed forces use dogs. Rescue workers and therapists of all kinds use dogs. A whole industry has grown up around our love of dogs, providing "designer" pet food, supplies, toys, and even clothing. There are dog walkers, dog day cares, dog spas, and professional groomers. Dogs occupy every corner of our lives. Everyone has seen one. Everyone knows what a dog is like.

Everyone knows what a wolf is. . .or do we?

Most of us think we have a pretty good idea of what a wolf is. We have seen wolves, usually in bit parts, in the movies. We have seen cartoons, photographs, and documentaries. We read about them in books and sometimes we see them in zoos.

Before we, the authors, began working with wolves, we thought we knew what wolves were, what they looked like, and basically how they lived. We have college degrees, after all, were generally interested in animals and watched documentaries on television. We had seen wolves, briefly, in zoos. Wolves looked like big dogs. They were gray, or "agouti." The ones that lived in "the Arctic" (wherever that was) were pure white. They all had yellow eyes. It was very simple.

Working at a wildlife facility, with real wolves, radically changed our views of what a wolf is. It also changed our attitude toward the sources of the information on which we had previously relied. Prior to working at Wolf Park, we "knew," through several documentaries, that wolves growl at their prey. We later found, through direct observation of many hunting wolves, that they almost never make threatening gestures, vocal or otherwise, toward prey. We also "knew," from the same documentaries, that the high-ranking alpha wolves always ate first. We found, again through direct observation over a period of years, that rank does not necessarily affect eating order. The things we thought we knew about wolves were continually challenged, and often refuted outright. Hey—where did all this information that we "knew" come from, anyway?

The wolf through a kaleidoscope

Pick any street in your town. Take a walk down it and randomly knock on twenty doors as you go by. Ask each individual what they think about wolves or wolf hybrids. You will likely hear twenty completely different answers.

Everyone brings their own opinions to the table, based on their own unique experiences, when thinking or speaking about wolves. In your hypothetical walk down the street you may meet people who will tell you:

- Wolves make great guard dogs.
- Wolves kill hundreds of sheep in a night.
- Wolves love children.
- Wolves eat children.
- Wolves weigh five hundred pounds.
- Wolves make great pets.
- Wolves are unpredictable and may kill you.

You may meet people who had wolves as pets while they were children and loved the animals dearly. You may meet people who were attacked by someone's pet wolf when they were children and now fear them. You may meet people whose neighbors had a wolf who ate neighborhood cats and chickens and had to be shot. You may meet people whose neighbors had a wolf who rescued a child. You may meet people who currently own wolves and use them as educational "ambassador" animals, taking them out to meet people to make them less fearful of wolves. And, unfortunately, you may meet people who own wolves and keep them on chains in the backyard as ferocious guard animals, defending their territory from passers by.

Likely all these different and contradictory anecdotes have some truth to them. Attacks by wolves on children have been documented just as thoroughly as the wild wolf's natural tendency to avoid people entirely when given the chance. Wolves have been seen to hunt and kill domestic stock, but an analysis of stomach contents indicate that livestock is not their primary food source. As we will see in future chapters, wolves exhibit enough variation in behavior that it's likely that every anecdote can find some supporting evidence somewhere. The thing to remember is that while a person may accurately describe something that actually happened once, there is a good chance that what they are describing is not necessarily the normal state of things. Just because there is one person, somewhere, who had X happen to them, there is a good chance that someone else will instead have Y (or Z or Q) happen to them in the same situation.

The baby elephant walk

The topic of wolves can be very touchy, mostly because "everybody knows" what a wolf is, and most people have developed very strong opinions about them. We're not here to make people angry. Right now, we just want to describe how people learn about things. Therefore, in order to demonstrate how people can reach their wildly different conclusions about wolves, we're not going to talk about wolves. We're going to talk about elephants.

A baby elephant walking. Photo courtesy of Sara Goldsmith, through Flickr Creative Commons.

Imagine walking into a pet store one afternoon and finding an adorable baby elephant in the window. "It's so cute!" your wife gushes as you watch the employees bottle-feed the elephant, bathe and powder it, and then put a little bow on its tail. It's tiny and friendly and follows you anywhere you go. On an impulse, you buy it, and it goes home with you. You tell all your neighbors about your elephant and they come over to see it and coo over it and take photos of themselves with it. You take photos of your children playing with it and post them on your web site.

Your elephant is very nice while it is young. It watches television in the living room and lets the children climb on its head. It sleeps in the closet, lives on lettuce and kitchen scraps, and keeps the bushes in your front yard neatly pruned.

Because of your positive experience with your elephant, you want to show other people how awesome elephants are. You take your elephant to nearby schools and introduce it to the students. You tell the children everything you know about elephants and let them feed your elephant apples and play with it. You show them there's nothing to be afraid of. The children all like your elephant. They give it pet names and tie bows on its tail.

Then your elephant starts to get older. It is too big for the children now and sometimes scares them. When they get scared, so does the elephant—who then defecates all over the place. It doesn't understand "doors" and keeps walking right through the walls. You try to train it, but it is hard to get the animal to listen to you. It is too big to visit schools anymore. It becomes too heavy for your floor and falls through into the basement. You chain it up outside.

Chained outside, the elephant becomes lonely and starts trumpeting incessantly. It gets bigger and bigger and it's getting more expensive to feed now. It needs hundreds of pounds of food daily and has destroyed your lawn and any vegetation it can reach. It needs heavy chains to hold it, and it is expensive to maintain, too. The children won't play with it anymore because it gets so excited when anyone comes near that it knocks them over with its trunk. The neighbors are complaining about the noise and the smell.

One day, while you are not home, your elephant accidentally injures a neighborhood child who is trying to feed it an apple. The elephant is so excited to see the child that it knocks him over and breaks his arm. The child's mother says the animal is vicious and attacked her child with no provocation and demands it be put down. The city investigates the situation and finds that you did not purchase the necessary permits for having an elephant and decides that the animal must be re-homed or destroyed. The animal shelter will not take an elephant, especially one that has injured a child. All the elephant rescues are full. Reluctantly, you have your elephant euthanized.

The next day, at the pet store, you see another beautiful baby elephant. Seeing how well-behaved it is, you decide the last one was "defective." You tell yourself that "The kids are older now. It will be different this time." And so you buy another elephant.

Thinking about this experience, what might you and other people involved say about elephants? You might say that the elephant made a great pet and was doing fine until the neighborhood kid messed things up and you were forced to put him down. Your spouse might say he got hard to handle when he got big and cost a lot of money to maintain. Your children may have completely different stories as well, depending on their relationships with the animal. Talk to the students in the schools you visited while you had the elephant and they'll probably say that elephants make wonderful pets. After all, your elephant was cute and well-behaved, ate apples out of their hands, and you had nothing but good things to say about it while you had it at their school. Talk to your neighbors and they may complain about the noise and the smell and how the elephant got loose one day and ate an entire bed of champion rosebushes, or stepped on their Poodle. The mother of the child injured by the elephant may tell you that elephants are dangerous, that they should not be kept as pets, and that under no account should they be allowed near children. The child and the doctor who treated the child's broken arm might agree. The elephant breeder who supplies the pet store probably has nothing but good things to say about elephants. He lives out in the country where no one minds the noise or the smell, and has a big facility to safely contain his elephants. He sends the babies away to pet stores and has never had any complaints from the stores.

The people at the local elephant rescue will likely say they are constantly dealing with people trying to surrender pet elephants after they start to cause problems. They may bemoan the actions of the breeders and pet stores, which continue to sell and promote the image of pet elephants, because elephants sell for a lot of money. An animal rights activist may tell you that elephants were simply not made to live in captivity, and there is no valid reason to keep an elephant in one's home, regardless of the animal's treatment, behavior, or circumstances. Alternatively, they may tell you that the only reason *which is beneficial to the elephant* to keep one captive is public education—not as a personal pet.

Having completed your interviews, you decide to do a little more research. You may discover that people living in rural villages in India, where villagers cooperate to train, keep, and feed elephants to do heavy work for the benefit of all, say that elephants are wonderful animals and hard workers and that it's perfectly normal to keep one or more in their village. However, people in Africa—where wild elephants often suddenly and aggressively invade villages and steal crop stores, trample fences, and knock over houses—generally view elephants as rampaging, possibly dangerous invaders, and would never consider keeping one as a pet.

Everyone encountering an elephant, even if they all meet the same elephant, forms a unique opinion based on their own experiences. The elephant's opinion, of course, is rarely considered in the equation, but that is a topic for another book.

Back to wolves

Now that we have gotten past the exciting part, we can start talking about wolves again. Go back and re-read the previous pages, replacing the word "elephant" with "wolf" as you go. In fact, one could replace "elephant" with "bear," "tiger," or "crocodile," or even "pig," "chicken," "cat," or "dog," because the concept holds broadly true for any animal, domestic or exotic. No matter what animal is the subject of the story, everyone is going to come out of the encounter with a sometimes slightly, sometimes radically, different point of view. We're all looking at the same elephant/bear/tiger/wolf, but you wouldn't know that from the descriptions you hear.

Complicating the general public's ability to form an accurate perception of wolves is the fact that most people do not actually personally encounter wolves very often. Their primary sources of information about wolves are generally the second-hand experiences they have had with wolves on television, in the movies, in books, and in talking to people (Karlsson and Sjöström, 2007). We may not even necessarily consciously gather this information. We do not need to actively be paying attention to something in order to mentally absorb it (Watanabe et al., 2001). It creeps in through the cracks, wrapped around other subjects. While we are not looking or paying attention, the impressions sit in our subconscious, waiting to reemerge once we start fishing in our brains for things related to the subject "wolf."

Wolves on TV and in movies

> *"Life imitates art more than art imitates life."*
> ~ Oscar Wilde

People these days get a lot of their information from visual media. Unfortunately, a lot of it, especially when it relates to wolves, is inaccurate. For example, many people have seen footage in documentaries (especially older ones) of wolves "hunting" deer. The camera first shows the deer running, with no wolves in the shot. Then it cuts away to a close-up shot of a wolf, growling and snarling, with its teeth bared and its hackles up. The wolf looks fierce and angry, as though it is really going to "get" those deer. The camera switches back to show the deer running again, then the screen goes black and some growling noises are played, and in the last scene the wolves are seen eating a deer.

Wolves are not camera shy, but the language barrier makes it difficult to get the true story. Photo courtesy of Monty Sloan.

This seemed logical to us when we first saw such footage many years ago on public television documentaries. We now know, through extensive personal observation, that wolves do not growl or bare their teeth at their prey. Those signals are used for threatening other wolves. Think about it—why would wolves want to threaten the deer? It would be like a human yelling at an ice cream cone before eating it. Ice cream cones do not speak "human" any more than deer speak "wolf." In reality, the creators of older documentaries could not find or film footage of wolves killing a deer, so instead they went out and shot footage of a deer running. Then they went somewhere else (likely a game farm which keeps captive exotic animals for photo shoots) and got footage of a wolf looking fierce, because that is what people who have not seen wolves hunt expect them to look like when they're hunting. They spliced the footage together to make a "hunt" which *looks* good, but is almost nothing like the real thing. Even modern documentaries still employ creative editing and writing to "enhance" the natural behavior of wolves to make it more interesting to the viewer. The real footage of wolves in the IMAX movie *Wolves* is cleverly edited together to form a story. While it succeeds in entertaining the viewing public, it does not necessarily accurately reflect events which normally occur in the wild.

Television shows and movies are still likely to err on the side of good entertainment as opposed to factual presentation. A fourth-season episode of *"Penn and Teller's B. S.!"* whose topic concerned people and their pets, opened with a close-up shot of a "wolf." The "wolf" in question was a calm, friendly-looking blue-eyed animal with a wide chest and a white mask—much more likely to be a low-content hybrid, or even a purebred husky, rather than a wolf. However, several million television viewers (and more via DVD) saw Penn Jillette introduce that animal, however facetiously, as a "face-eating wolf." That image of a "wolf" will now live silently in their brains, ready to affect—consciously or not—everything they think about wolves.

The movie industry has contributed significantly to the misinformation surrounding wolves. Dogs or wolf hybrids are frequently cast as wolves in such a way that both their looks and behaviors are depicted inaccurately. Whether a wolf in a film is cast as a loyal side-kick, defending his human friends and nobly rescuing people from the dangers of the wild—or as the villain, stalking and terrorizing the film's heroine—its behavior is not representative of the real thing.

"Two Socks," a wolf in the movie *Dances With Wolves,* was played by two animals (billed as pure wolves) which do indeed look like wolves. But the behavior of Two Socks (making friends with, and later protecting, Kevin Costner's character) was highly unusual for a pure wolf. The film ascribed *human* motives to the animal and while it made for great viewing and an excellent story, it was not a realistic picture of animal behavior. The behavior (and, to some extent, the looks) of *White Fang* in the novel and movie of the same name—about a high-content wolf hybrid who lived among wolves and then among humans—did contain some natural behaviors, though they were thoroughly altered for entertainment value. For example, when a lone wolf pup was introduced to a "pack" of dog pups, he consistently ended up at the bottom of the pecking order. In reality, given that a wolf matures more quickly and generally has a higher drive for dominance than a dog, he would be very unlikely to lose wrestling matches with dog pups of the same age. The book and movie *Never Cry Wolf*—about a naturalist studying Arctic wolves to see if they were killing local caribou—did contain some accurate depictions of natural behavior, but both were also "edited for publication" (especially the movie, made by Disney), gently twisted to show more story than realism.

It is almost impossible to find video media in which a wolf exhibits its natural behavior. Natural wolf behavior—running and hiding from people—is too *boring* to appear in modern cinema. Far too often wolves are used in film in ways which simply reinforce a person's already formed perceptions of them, playing up either the romanticized or demonized impression that their target audience likely already believes. Tragically, this phenomenon is not limited merely to television and movies. Nearly all entertainment media dramatizes or "enhances" wolf behavior in some way to make it more entertaining.

Wolves in popular literature

> *"Be careful about reading health books. You may die of a misprint."*
> ~ Mark Twain

Popular literature about wolves is often no better than documentaries and movies. Writers are wonderful people and many go to great lengths to get their facts straight, but sometimes their research is not entirely thorough, or their focus is more on entertainment than fact. This results in books which impart questionable wolf "knowledge."

Many of us grew up reading stories of the Wild West, and are familiar with the legends of wolves with names like Lobo, Old Lefty, Big Foot, or Three-Toes, who would terrorize ranchers for years before finally being brought down by the Good Guy at the end of the book (Coleman, 2006; Hampton, 1997). These stories made for rousing tales told around a campfire, but once subjected to the "telephone game" of being passed verbally from person to person, have tended to lose whatever accuracy they may have originally had with each retelling. Today's stories—of a wolf killing $50,000 worth of cattle over the space of three years, for example—are fantastic in every sense (Gipson, 1998). In some cases, the skulls or pelts of these animals have been preserved, but careful analysis reveals a few inconsistencies in the stories as they are currently told. In fact, some of these great "wolves" may even have been dogs, coyotes, or hybrids.

Each new school year, Wolf Park receives several calls from teachers who have started an instructional session on wolves by having their students read *Julie of the Wolves*, by Jean Craighead George. The book concerns a young lady named Miyax who is running away from her Eskimo settlement in Alaska trying to reach her pen pal in San Francisco (who calls her Julie, hence the book's title). Along the way Miyax gets lost and is "adopted" by a pack of Arctic wolves who help her to survive. While the author was a naturalist who had actually visited Denali National Park and observed wild wolves, she was not a professional wolf behaviorist (this is probably fortunate, as wolf behaviorists are not often also good children's book writers!). The book contains many descriptions of wolf behavior, some of them accurate, some of them fanciful. The primary thing to remember is that the story itself is a work of fiction. Its purpose is to tell an interesting tale about a girl on the Alaskan tundra and her relationship with her family, but not to accurately describe wolf behavior. While the book is an excellent introduction to wolves, portraying them as intelligent, generally benign animals, the book is not a good foundation for acquiring a strong grasp of real wolf behavior.

Books for younger children almost always turn away from the factual in favor of what is funny, more understandable, or more symbolic or representative of something other than a real wolf. This makes perfectly good sense, as not every child is ready to learn about, say, hunting behavior and its eventual outcome, death. What is important is to remember that these books are *stories* first and factual descriptions second. Generally, real wolf behavior (seeing a human and immediately running away, or eating cute fluffy bunnies) does not make for a good children's book. One should assume that some liberties have been taken in order to make the book more acceptable, or more interesting, to both parents and children.

"Grown-up" literature is, unfortunately, subject to the same trends. Wolf behavior is woven, often incidentally, into an otherwise unrelated story, appearing as an interesting anecdote. In the absence of further background information, the behaviors described in these books may be accepted by the reader as fact simply because the rest of the book seems so factual or so well-researched. The *Earth's Children* novels by Jean M. Auel, featuring the Cro-Magnon woman Ayla and her tame prehistoric animals including a wolf, horse, and cave lion, is primarily a romance centering around Ayla, not an academic review of animal behavior. However, the seemingly well-researched nature of the books and their vivid, detailed descriptions of prehistoric human behavior may lead a reader to unconsciously accept their descriptions of wolf behavior as fact, even though they are largely inaccurate. (No doubt professors of archaeology and sociology, other topics incidentally covered by this series, also bemoan the lack of a bold disclaimer on the covers of these books stating, "This is a work of fiction.")

Not all literature is pure fiction, of course, and there are several non-fiction books available describing an author's life with his or her wolf (*Wolves at Our Door*), wolf hybrid (*Kavika: Tales of a Timber Wolf*), lion *(Born Free),* elephant *(Modoc),* snowy owl *(Wesley the Owl),* etc. Some of these present very accurate behavioral information— but, in general, these works are designed to be *entertaining*, and are not written, or even intended to be written, from a scientifically accurate point of view. Most of the authors have only interacted with the individual animal(s) described in the book (not a sufficient sample size), and the books present long and fascinating anecdotes more than scientifically accurate analyses of animal behavior.

For example, Charlie, star of the popular "Daily Coyote" blog (as well as its spinoff book, *The Daily Coyote*) entertains thousands of visitors with tales (and breathtaking photos) of life with a coyote. The blog's author, Shreve Stockton, does actually present a pretty good picture of what *her* life with a coyote is like but, as *one* person raising *one* coyote in *one* location, Ms. Stockton is not personally *experiencing* a complete picture of what it can be like to raise a coyote. She is not intentionally leaving facts out, nor is she being intentionally misleading in any way, but she certainly cannot comment on things which she has not encountered, and about which she is unaware.

We notice that since the Daily Coyote blog has become popular, it appears now that "everybody knows" someone who has raised a coyote as a pet. Charlie's story is unique and certainly not representative of all people who have ever tried to raise a coyote pup, but because of the publicity, everything that happens with Charlie is sneaking into our collective consciousness as "this is what happens when you raise a baby coyote." (For a brief note on coyotes and coydogs, please see Appendix A.)

The talking heads

> *"Television is called a medium because anything good on it is rare."*
> ~ Fred Allen, comedian

Adding to the muddle of "facts" is the rise of the "entertainment expert"—someone who can tell a really good story about animals yet actually knows very little about the animals involved. Because their on-screen speech may sound quite knowledgeable (and in fact may be written by other, real experts), these "talking heads" can be mistaken for people who actually understand the animals concerned and who apply a decent scientific background to their statements. Television personalities of all sorts have long been mistaken for experts in the topics chosen and penned for them by their writers, or simply on the basis of their being famous (consider talk show hosts such as Oprah, being asked for their opinion on presidential candidates). Today, the phenomenon is even worse, as publicists and marketers take people with dubious scientific backgrounds and plaster them all over the front page labeled as "experts" because they provide a quotable sound bite or look good on film.

An example of this phenomenon at work is Shaun Ellis. Ellis is an amateur researcher and wolf enthusiast who was hired by a wildlife park in Devon, England, to hand-raise some wolf pups which had been abandoned by their mother. Apparently, solely on the basis of his experience with this single litter of pups, Ellis has been popularly named an "expert" in wolf behavior, despite the fact that we can find no evidence of any scientific education in his background (according to a 2007 article by Bob Brown of ABC News, Ellis never finished high school), and his behavioral work with wolves appears to have been nearly entirely self-guided. Media interviews and articles skim over any academic experience he may have, and cite his wolf background as having "moved through Idaho and Canada" during his youth or "lived with" the Nez Perce Indians in Idaho. In an April 2007 newspaper interview with Luaine Lee of the McClatchy-Tribune News Service, Ellis admits, "Having a science background or applying it to science would be something we didn't need to do."

While it is certainly not necessary to have an advanced degree in order to know something about wolves, this lack of scientific background seems to have resulted in some unusual assumptions about wolf behavior. For example, in his 2006 book, *Spirit of the Wolf*, Ellis asserts—among some admittedly otherwise good facts—that the alpha female starts a hunt "by adjusting the position of her tail...(and) excret[ing] an odor which tells the pack which way to turn." We have not found this behavior documented in any scientific studies, and nothing we have seen over years of experience and communication with others has indicated that the alpha female, or any other wolf, uses its tail as a pheromone-based "turn signal" of any sort. While we feel that Ellis is doing an admirable job getting the general public interested in wolves, by including such unverified "facts" in his books, he is failing regrettably to give his audience an accurate picture.

Consider dog trainer Cesar Millan, also with no scientific background or formal education with regard to animal behavior (according to his own web site). Millan is now the "expert" responsible for educating millions of dog owners concerning the behavior and training of their pets. As far as we can tell, he appears to base his training methods on the popular (but not scientifically accurate) image of the behavior of a wolf pack, telling people to "be the pack leader" and exert dominance over their dogs through a regimen of exercise, enforcement of rules, and intimidation. We feel that this methodology, while appearing to be highly effective *in the hands of Mr. Millan,* can also be potentially dangerous in untrained hands who may not fully understand how what they are doing affects a dog's behavior or their own personal safety (in fact, the disclaimer on his TV show basically says just that). Millan has a lot of correct ideas. Unfortunately, his teaching style appears to us to be likely to result in the potential for some sad misunderstandings, as we do not always find that his explanations of why his methods succeed accurately reflect the real mechanisms at work.

Likewise, Jim and Jamie Dutcher, who produced an award-winning documentary and several books (including *Wolves at Our Door*) on the subject of living with a pack of captive wolves in the wilderness of Idaho, appear to us to be filmmakers first and behaviorists second. Their portrayal of wolves is positive and excellent and, again, they are on the front lines in the fight to get people interested in and involved with wolves. However, their narratives fall short of accurate representations of wolf behavior in favor of the story they are telling, and their facts can get shaky in areas where they simply do not seem to have the scientific background to understand what is going on.

Even people who might be legitimately considered to be experts may have significant gaps in their knowledge—especially as it relates to wolves and wolf hybrids. A brief online search of the curricula of several popular veterinary schools reveals that not one contains even a single class called "Identifying Wolf Hybrids," and yet veterinarians are routinely called in to lend an "expert" opinion in such matters. Veterinarians, dog trainers, and animal shelter employees are often assumed to have a high level of experience with wolves and wolf behavior even when they may have no experience at all. Most of these people will not abuse their position as "experts" and will not offer advice on topics about which they have no firsthand knowledge. However, enough of them do so (or are coerced into doing so) that their variably accurate opinions have emerged in the common consciousness as "fact."

"They" may say it, but it still isn't true

> *"I know that you believe you understand what you think I said, but I'm not sure you realize that what you heard is not what I meant."*
>
> ~ Robert McCloskey, author

Perhaps the most prolific source of misinformation about wolves and hybrids comes from individuals who are not trying to push or sell anything at all—they are simply one's well-meaning friend or neighbor, or just "that guy down the street" who owns (or thinks he owns) a wolf. Frequently, these are people who believe they have spent a great deal of time working with one or more wolves or wolf hybrids, but who have in reality been handling pure dogs. A popular story at Wolf Park concerned a man, met by one of the Park staff, who was running his own wildlife park based around a pack of Malamutes which he firmly believed were wolves, and were advertised to be wolves. Ironically, he was giving the public who visited his facility accurate information about wolves and was treating his animals exactly as though they were wolves, using wolf-appropriate containment and husbandry methods. So, in that sense he was acting as a source of good information. Unfortunately, the animals he displayed were still Malamutes, and his related experiences with their behavior and husbandry would not make a good reference foundation for someone wanting to open a wolf sanctuary or to work with real wolves.

Likewise, some people use inaccurate information to arrive at the conclusion that their personal companion animal is a wolf when in fact it is a dog. They may even perform public education programs with the animal, intending only to show that wolves are gentle, curious animals who do not mean any harm. These dogs will likely enjoy long and happy lives as ambassadors to the public, and the owners will enjoy extra attention from friends and neighbors as they regale the curious with adventurous tales of how exciting it is to raise such an animal. The real danger in this situation is twofold. First, because these people are presenting a dog as a wolf, they contribute heavily to the misinformation already discussed in this chapter, since the behavior exhibited by the dog is unlikely to accurately represent the behavior of a pure wolf. Second, their apparent ownership of a "wolf" reinforces their position as an "expert," and they become an instant source of "fact" to any curious individual, even though they do not actually own a wolf.

We do not wish to imply that the directors, the trainers, the writers, the owners, or the veterinarians mentioned above are entirely wrong, or that they are deliberately spreading misinformation. At heart, they generally really do want to be telling, and are trying to tell, the truth. Indeed much of what they say or write or portray may indeed be composed of factual, useful information. These people are simply victims of the natural, but misguided, assumption by the public that, because these experts are experts on topic *a*, they are also experts on topics *b, c,* and *d*. Or that, having seen or owned *one* wolf, one can make extrapolations to *all* wolves. Unfortunately, the many real facts that these people and media outlets do present can make inaccurate assertions even harder to spot, especially if one does not already have a strong background in wolf behavior.

Recommended sources of information

Fortunately, there are still good places to learn about wolves, dogs, and hybrids. Our alma mater, Wolf Park (www.wolfpark.org) is an excellent place to start, with nearly forty years of experience working with socialized captive wolves. It regularly offers seminars on a variety of wolf and dog-related topics. Many other centers also work with wolves and are great sources of information (see more recommendations in Appendix B.) We have also listed a number of books in the Recommended Reading section which are excellent. Probably the best in-print book for the layman is *Wolves: Behavior, Ecology and Conservation,* edited by Mech and Boitani. There are also a number of internet forums of various dog and wolf hybrid groups that provide well run forums for discussion among experienced owners of such animals, many with a strong factual background and a very realistic perception of just what kind of animal is living in their home. The "Wolf Dunn," at http://www.inetdesign.com/wolfdunn/, is an excellent place to start searching for these.

Four wolves on a fallen tree trunk at Wolf Park. Photo courtesy of Monty Sloan.

There are many zoos and rescue organizations which educate people about wolves, and most institutions are happy to answer questions. However, some facilities have more experience than others and are better able to give an accurate picture of wolf behavior. In general, the more time a facility has spent working with wolves, the more publicly accessible it is (does it give tours or presentations?), the larger the number of wolves it has handled (has it only ever had one wolf, or has it seen hundreds of wolves over the years?), and the more often it works with other wolf facilities, the more accurate its information will be. Remember, variance comes on a number of axes, and the more experience a person or facility has, involving more individual animals, people, and situations, the more detailed and thorough will be their mental map of wolves and wolf behavior.

As you investigate the various resources available, you will notice that not all of them agree on all points concerning the wolf. Even experts disagree, so simply consulting one facility or one individual is unlikely to give a complete picture. This is why we stress that it is so difficult for someone who has not spent years consulting with a huge variety of informational sources to put together a mental image of the wolf comprehensive enough to make snap decisions on the ancestry of a rescue animal. Even people who *have* invested the time and energy are sometimes missing pieces of the puzzle.

In conclusion

It seems that a person's view of the nature of the wolf depends mainly on what one has heard or read, to whom one has been speaking, and what experiences one has recently had with wolves. The poor elephant mentioned in our example was docile, tractable, friendly, cute, good with kids, and trainable, while at the same time vicious, dangerous, messy, unpredictable, expensive, and impossible to live with. Our simplistic elephant story above does not even take into account possible variations in the innate behavior of animals: no two animals are exactly alike. One hypothetical owner might have his hands on a specimen which is idiosyncratically intrinsically tame, while his neighbor may end up with a genuinely obnoxious, possibly aggressive individual.

Developing an expertise in wolves requires having encountered not just one, or two, or even ten wolves, but a large number of wolves and in a wide variety of situations. A wolf in a zoo or in a rescue facility will be a very different wolf than one living in a suburban home, a private wildlife park, or in the wild. They will behave differently, and their behavior will be perceived differently, than wolves found in other situations and with other people. Having experience with many wolves, in many situations, results in the formation of a mental map of "average" wolf behavior when encountered in a variety of "average" wolf situations. While there will always be exceptions, this map can guide an individual to make highly informed guesses about what average Wolf A will do when placed in average Situation B. No one can say for certain what any wolf placed in any situation will do, but knowing a great deal about the many axes upon which wolves vary can allow one to paint an accurate picture of what most wolves are like, and to give a good guess about what this particular wolf might do when placed in this particular situation.

There is no single, platonic form of "wolf," no archetypal animal with a single list of properties that all wolves necessarily possess. There is no universal, all-encompassing "wolf." Wolves vary. Coming under the heading of "wolf" is a huge variety of animals, some dangerous, some benign, some midway between the two, varying on a thousand different axes, many dependent upon the humans or situations with which they are paired. This forces us to move away from writing some universal law ("All wolves are friendly" or "All wolves are dangerous") and requires judging each situation individually, with reference to the qualities of the animal at hand, its potential owner or placement location, and the circumstances in which both reside.

Chapter 2
So What Are Wolves and Dogs Really Like?

"The truth is rarely pure and never simple."
~ Oscar Wilde

The many people all seeing different sides of the same elephant in the previous chapter missed out on one unique problem which occurs when working with wolves and dogs: nobody above the age of five or so can mistake an elephant for anything else. Wolves, however, are so closely related to the dog that dogs are routinely mistaken for wolves and vice versa. Hybrids, which can look and act like either animal, are particularly problematic to identify. This complicates the "elephant" analogy hopelessly with people who *think* they have owned, or seen, or been mauled by an elephant but who have actually encountered a misidentified hippopotamus.

The difficulties in telling "wolf" from "dog" are huge, but surmounting them starts with having some idea of what a "wolf" is, and what a "dog" is. In this chapter, we focus on describing the physical and behavioral characteristics of the wolf and the dog, emphasizing the primary differences between them. *Similarities* between wolves and dogs are still so pronounced that dogs have, after hundreds of years of being considered a distinct species, been recently reclassified as a subspecies of wolf (Wilson and Reeder, 1993). Debates, of course, continue on this subject as we will also mention later.

The wolf: Born to be wild

"Wolves are very resourceful. All they need to survive is for people not to shoot them."
~ Bob Ferris, Defenders of Wildlife

The wolf is a wild animal. This means that for millions of years it has been under evolutionary pressures which have adapted it perfectly for its role as one of the top predators in the food chain. Wolves are born with certain basic physical and mental accoutrements for their role as a cooperative social predator: a body which will grow to be long and lean and muscular; long, strong legs for running great distances; sharp, strong teeth with which to grab and hold prey and, later, to dissect it; powerful jaws to guide those teeth; and a comparatively large brain, the better to analyze prey movements and behavior, pay attention to signals from other wolves, prey, and the outside world, and to form strategies to capture prey as well as to interact with other wolves.

Wolves are also born with a toolkit of reflexes and motor patterns which are genetically based. They are born knowing how to howl, how to stalk, catch, and attempt to kill prey, techniques which are refined through learning as the animals get older. They also come with a basic repertoire of social behaviors (food begging, whining, licking, growling, biting) with which to interact and get along with their littermates and parents. Learning also refines and alters the contents of this behavioral toolkit as the animal gets older.

The ideal cooperative social predator. Photo courtesy of Monty Sloan.

Consider the wolf as an animal that, more or less, was created by nature to live without depending on man. The wild wolf is under constant environmental pressures to feed itself, keep itself safe and healthy, and to reproduce. These pressures have affected which genes a wolf can safely express. Wolves with slight deviations from the norm (a little more or less aggressive, or having a longer tail or smaller ears) can generally survive because these small deviations do not prevent them from feeding themselves or reproducing. However, a wolf with a significant deviation from the norm (weighing only twenty pounds as an adult, or having a head too big to fit through the birth canal) would have major trouble meeting these basic requirements and would likely not survive long enough to reproduce. This strong environmental pressure has kept wolves pretty much to a "cookie-cutter" standard. While they do exhibit remarkable variation in both behavior and looks, they are generally very similar to each other (especially compared to the dog) because they are all under roughly the same pressures from their environment, and these pressures are very strong.

The dog (Canis familiaris, Canis lupus familiaris)

"Yesterday I was a dog. Today I'm a dog. Tomorrow I'll probably still be a dog. Sigh! There's so little hope for advancement."

~ Snoopy

The dog is what happens when humans, through selective breeding, alter the environmental pressures on the wolf and change the looks and behavior any individual animal can safely express. Each one of the many and varied breeds of dogs is descended from wolves (Vilà, C. et al., 1997), the result of years of pressures which are not the same as those in the wild. (This is not the *complete* story, as we will mention later, but it is a good way of looking at it for now.)

A Chihuahua. Photo by Jessica Addams.

Dogs are domesticated animals. This means that for thousands of generations (estimates vary) they have been under selective pressures which have adapted them for living comfortably with humans. Each newborn dog puppy is descended from generations of ancestors who lived and worked well with humans, and carries their genes.

Because of his or her genetic makeup, every newborn dog puppy is very likely to get along well with humans. A wolf puppy, by contrast, has no ancestors who lived among humans and no genes coding for characteristics which make him or her specifically suitable to live with humans.

This is the primary difference separating dogs from wolves. All dog puppies are born with thousands of years of genetic "tuning" to make them "good with people." Wolf puppies are born with thousands of years of genetic "tuning" which make them "good social hunters." This difference between being programmed to be "good with people" versus being programmed to be "good social hunters" is where wolf and dog first, and primarily, diverge. In Chapter 3, we will cover the process of domestication by which it became advantageous for some wolves to work well with people, and how selecting solely for being "good with people" may have given rise to all of the other ways that dogs differ from their wolf ancestors. But for now, keep the concepts of "good with people" and "good social hunters" in focus as you read the rest of this chapter.

Physical characteristics and varieties of the wolf

Wolves range in weight from 70 to 120 pounds. Individual animals living in desert environments tend toward the lower end of the range while those in areas with colder weather and a lot of snow tend toward the higher end of the range. They are approximately twenty-six to thirty-two inches tall at the shoulder and about five to six feet long from nose to tail tip—about the size of a big German Shepherd. They are born with blue eyes, but as adults their eyes turn yellow, gold, or orange, or sometimes a pale yellow-green. Their tails are straight and do not curl over the back as is seen in the Siberian Husky and Malamute. Wolves are generally *agouti* colored, with fur banded in black, tan, and white, but their fur can come in any shade from white to black. Fur color does not affect behavior or personality, and pups of all colors can be born in the same litter. Although black wolves can have patches of white on their chest, muzzle, or feet, wolves do not come in "spotted" varieties with large patches of white on their bodies.

Three wolves, all unique in color and body shape. Photo courtesy of Monty Sloan.

Wolves have one breeding cycle per year, and neither sex is fertile outside of the breeding season. Exact dates can vary depending on geographical location, but generally mating occurs in late January or February and the pups are born sixty-one to sixty-three days later, in late April or early May (Seal et al., 1979). The average litter size is two to six. The pups emerge from the den around four to six weeks of age. They will reach ninety percent of their adult size by the end of their first year.

When we speak of "wolves" in this book, we refer primarily to "gray wolves," *Canis lupus*. "Wolves" do come in different "flavors," or subspecies, of course, just like dogs come in breeds. The current list of subspecies of the gray wolf varies as scientists learn more about the population genetics of wolves. Today, there are generally considered to be five subspecies of wolves in North America: the Arctic wolf (*Canis lupus arctos*); the eastern, or eastern timber wolf (*C. l. lycaon*); the great plains, timber, or buffalo wolf (*C. l. nubilus*); the northwestern, Rocky Mountain, or McKenzie Valley wolf (*C. l. occidentalis*); and the Mexican gray wolf (*C. l. baileyi*). Since the distinctions between subspecies seem to be a matter of personal preference on the part of individual researchers, and reclassifications take place every few years, there is not a need to be overly concerned with the variation between the subspecies.

A Mexican gray wolf. Photo by Jessica Addams.

Beyond the gray wolf, the wolf variations one is most likely to encounter in the United States are the Arctic wolf, the Mexican gray wolf, and the red wolf (*Canis rufus*), which is not actually a subspecies of gray wolf, but another species of wolf altogether. Keeping things brief, the Arctic wolf is, of course, a wolf with white fur (and dark, pigmented skin, differentiating it from an albino animal). The Mexican gray wolf looks like a gray wolf, but with longer fur. The red wolf looks much like a coyote, with shorter, redder fur than a gray wolf. The Arctic wolf is reasonably common in captivity and does not differ significantly from "standard" gray wolves other than through its striking coloration.

A juvenile black-phase gray wolf and a juvenile Arctic/gray wolf cross, which looks much like its Arctic parent. Photo courtesy of Monty Sloan.

The important thing for rescue professionals to know about the Mexican gray wolf and the red wolf is that they are both critically, unimaginably endangered, with only about one hundred individuals of each species living in the wild and a small, carefully managed population living in captivity. Mexican gray wolves live wild only in a small portion of Arizona and New Mexico. Red wolves live wild only in two tiny refuge areas in northeastern North Carolina according to the US Fish and Wildlife Service. For a private individual to have possession of one of these animals, or a hybrid of a dog and one of these animals, is almost beyond the scope of comprehension, making any "red wolf" or "Mexican wolf" hybrids encountered by a rescue professional highly, highly suspect.

Physical characteristics of the dog

Physical characteristics vary widely between dog breeds—there are dogs with short legs, dogs with long legs, dogs with curly and straight tails, dogs with long muzzles and flat faces, dogs with eyes of all colors, dogs with long coats and dogs with short coats, etc. Scientists have made much of how "plastic," or changeable, dog genetics is—after all, roughly the same genetic code is producing animals as different as the Toy Poodle and the Afghan Hound. Dogs can look like anything, from a teacup Yorkie to a German Shepherd—and note that "anything" *does* include the wolf. After all, the wolf is the original "template" for the dog. It's logical then that some dogs would turn out still looking like the original template, notably breeds like the Alaskan Malamute and Siberian Husky.

A Shar-Pei. Photo courtesy of Monty Sloan.

Compared to wolves—who, as mentioned before, do not show great variation in size and shape—dogs range in size from the Chihuahua to the Newfoundland. Head shape also varies tremendously, from the flat-faced Bulldog and Japanese Chin to dogs with prominent muzzles like the Borzoi and Bull Terrier. Some breeds look so different from each other that it is hard to imagine that they belong to the same species of animal. Under the heading "dog" come animals as varied as Pomeranians, Border Collies, Greyhounds, Beagles, and Xoloitzcuintli (a hairless breed whose ancestry traces back to the Aztecs). The amount of individual variation is significant between breeds—and even among individuals of only one breed—and is still highly noticeable. For example, Labradors come in black, chocolate, and yellow colors. Poodles come in "toy," "standard," and "giant" sizes. German Shepherds come in various bloodlines which produce huge, lean, long-bodied individuals, all-white individuals, long-haired individuals, or small, muscular, beefy individuals.

A Brittany Spaniel. Photo by Jessica Addams.

Usually, female dogs come into heat, or estrous, two times a year, at any time of year. Male dogs are generally fertile all year round. Litter size depends on the size of the dog in question, but generally tends to be larger than litters of wolves. Puppies can be born year round (although gestation is still approximately sixty-two days, like the wolf).

Behavioral characteristics of the wolf

"Koani's a good wolf, but she's a really bad dog."
~ Pat Tucker, Wild Sentry

As a whole, wolves in the wild are under significant environmental pressure every day to be independent, intelligent, ambitious animals whose primary goals are obtaining food, rising in social rank, and defending territory which includes one's food, one's sleeping space, and potential mates. These factors form the basis of wolf behavior. Wolves also have other goals, and some wolves are less focused on their goals than are others, but most are pretty intensely focused upon food, rank, and territory. In the wild, wolves who are persistent enough to obtain these things survive, and are able to successfully reproduce, period. The wolves who don't fight for their food, rank, and territory don't get food, rank, or territory. Therefore, we don't see a lot of their offspring as a result.

It's not all hard work all the time. Photo courtesy of Monty Sloan.

Wolves need a pretty big brain, compared to dogs, in order to accomplish all these goals in the wild. They need to be able to pick out the one elk with a suspicious limp, to avoid flying bison hooves and horns, and to not eat dangerous things like snakes or porcupines. They need to be able to keep a careful eye on other wolves and watch for the "opportune moment" to sneak in and snatch a potential mate, a bit of food, or a higher rank, and to be aware when other wolves are planning such a move on them. They need to be able to track prey in snow and on rocks and in sand, to avoid inclement weather, and to avoid humans. Wolves pay a lot of attention to their environment and are constantly analyzing it for patterns and testing its boundaries.

This highly developed intelligence makes for animals which don't generally get along well living in human society. Their brains are designed to process vast amounts of information about their prey and their pack mates. They are not designed to sit on a sofa or be a lap ornament all day. Consequently, wolves get bored easily and don't like living in a single small space, such as a house, without a lot of intellectual input. With no proper release for their various drives, they are likely to become destructive or aggressive, turn into escape artists, or otherwise exhibit "sub-optimal" behavior for a household pet.

Exhibiting these behaviors does not mean that these animals are innately vicious, aggressive, unpredictable, or "bad." Natural wolf behavior is adapted for implementation *in the wild*, not in the human home. It's only when the wild behavior is exhibited in a "tame" human environment that it looks out of place and/or dangerous. As Pat Tucker says in the quote above, these animals are perfectly good wolves. They just make really bad dogs.

Wolf social groups and packs

Wolves live in social groups called packs, which are generally family groups "led" by a mature breeding pair of high rank, including some lower-ranking young from previous years, and with the most recent year's litter lowest in rank. The exact mechanics of rank order are not completely understood (and are sometimes completely *mis*understood), but generally moxie, skill, attitude, and ambition (rather than just age, size, or strength, although those contribute as well) bring a wolf to the top. Although low-ranking animals have been known to mate and bear pups without leaving their natal pack (pack of birth), the higher an animal is in rank and thus the higher degree of social freedom it enjoys, the more likely that it will be able to form a new pack and successfully breed and rear young. Attaining a rank high enough to successfully reproduce is generally an important part of a wild wolf's survival strategy.

A group of wolves within a pack greeting one another. Photo courtesy of Monty Sloan.

In the wild, resources are scarce, and wolves naturally protect resources such as food, a favorite sleeping location, a den, or a potential mate, from scavengers and from each other. Territorial displays include scent-marking of territory, scraping with the feet, howling to drive away other packs, and growling or biting to defend food, sleeping space, or other favored possessions.

A mature wolf greeting a pup. Photo courtesy of Monty Sloan.

Wolves cooperate to obtain food and rear pups. To accomplish these goals, and minimize conflict while doing so, they communicate through a series of complex behaviors—mostly body language, sounds, and smells. Some of these signals can be quite difficult for human observers to see—eye or body movements which pass quickly or are very subtle, sounds made quietly, or scents that humans cannot detect. Aggression is generally highly ritualized, and involves posturing and threats rather than damaging attacks. Especially in the wild, wolves have nothing to gain by killing their pack mates in fights.

Wolf pups, when they are very young, behave much like dogs. They are friendly, curious animals, engaging in a great deal of developmental play behavior (wrestling, tag, tug-of-war), without undue emphasis on rank order or territoriality. Around the age of two, however, wolves typically reach sexual maturity. At this point, they begin to manifest the behavior of an adult animal, with an emphasis on hunting, territoriality, and achieving high enough rank to reproduce. At this age, young wolves are likely to leave their natal pack and begin to search for a lone member of the opposite sex with which to start their own pack (their best chance of survival and reproduction).

The drive for rank in wolves

In order to achieve social harmony in a pack, wolves adopt a rank order, a sort of "ladder" of rank in which each wolf has a place either higher or lower on the totem pole than any other wolf. This allows wolves to use a sort of "shorthand" when interacting over a sleeping place or other coveted item, so every little disagreement does not need to be settled with teeth and claws. With everyone knowing who has previously proven themselves higher ranking, through whatever means, lower-ranking wolves may choose to simply cede resources to higher-ranking wolves without more than a token display of potential aggression (as subtle as a brief direct stare) from the higher-ranking animal. This minimizes the necessity of pulling out all the stops, and risking potential major damage, by actually fighting over small things.

A lower-ranking wolf voluntarily rolls over and submits to a higher-ranking wolf. Wolves generally do not forcibly pin or "alpha roll" each other to show dominance. Photo courtesy of Monty Sloan.

Much fuss has been made, especially in the media, over wolf rank order, often comparing it to aspects of human society. The reality is much more complex and not fully understood, but the basic ideas are clear. The rank order is not assigned, nor is it some sort of template wolf packs must fill. Rather, it arises naturally from family structure (Mech, 1999). Generally, a wolf pack is formed when a pair of lone wolves mate and have a litter. The two adult animals, by simple virtue of their age, become the highest ranking animals (the "alpha pair") by default when the pups are born. Young wolves do not generally get their pubertal hormone burst and start focusing on rising in rank until their second winter or so, and often another litter has been born in that time. Thus, most wild wolf packs consist of an alpha, or breeding pair, dominant by dint of age and experience and of simply having *been* alpha for as long as their offspring can remember, along with a host of lower-ranking, younger wolves, usually between the ages of one and three, who simply have not yet left to form a new pack (Mech et al., 1998). The young from the most recent litter are on the bottom of the rank order simply because they are so young (Mech, 1970; Haber, 1977; Murie, 1985).

Controversy has arisen concerning the study of rank order in wolves. To some extent, this is due to the fact that wild and captive wolves display different intensities of dominance behavior. These differences, which can be subtle or confusing, are sometimes ignored in popular media. Wild packs, as mentioned above, generally consist of a single adult pair with a number of related juveniles who have not yet dispersed, while in captivity a pack may consist of a number of unrelated adult individuals, with no option to disperse. The result is that there can be a higher level of tension and a greater number of high intensity displays of aggression in a captive wolf pack compared to a pack of wolves in the wild. Therefore, studies of dominance or rank order in a captive pack may not reveal data which applies to wild wolves (Mech, 1999). In fact, wild wolves seem to have a much less rigid rank order, into which they put less visible effort, than do captive wolves (Schenkel, 1947; Rabb et al., 1967; Zimen, 1975, 1982; Lockwood 1979). Unfortunately, since wild wolves have historically been so difficult to study long-term, most work has been done using captive packs as models, and so many assumptions about wolf behavior may well be wrong when considering the behavior of natural wolf packs. However, this is not entirely relevant to the subject at hand: our focus here is on how wolves, both in the wild and in captivity, exhibit greater intensity of behavior than do dogs, and not on the exact mechanics of wolf behavior.

Rank among wolves is not like rank in the human military. Wolves are not "born into" a rank (the puppy of an alpha pair is not necessarily going to be alpha when he grows up), and rank is not guaranteed or given at a particular age or after some sort of accomplishment (Zimen, 1976). Rank is surprisingly flexible. Rank order can shift in a moment, on the basis of a single, spectacular fight. Or it can shift slowly, over months or years, as an older animal ages or a lower ranking animal gains confidence and uses repeated, opportunistic, ritualized testing to wear down another animal's ability to stand up to it. Two animals, especially younger animals, can have approximately equal rank, "sharing" a spot on the ladder until one decides he or she has had enough and settles the matter. Two animals can also *never* argue over rank, and coexist peacefully their whole lives. Rank can also be circular, with animal A dominant to animal B, who is dominant to animal C, who is dominant to animal A.

Rank may be ignored during feeding, where sometimes a low ranking animal can displace a high ranking animal from a food item. It can also reverse during times of play, as a high ranking animal allows a lower-ranking animal to "win," at least temporarily, a wrestling match. Rank may also matter less during the plentiful, quiet summer months of puppy-raising than it does during the food-scarce winter months when the reproductive season looms large on the horizon. Animals have even been known to "swap" ranks, with a low ranking animal rising during the summer months and returning to its former position the following winter. Essentially, rank order is less a "code" or set of rules that the wolves follow than it is a system of organization that *humans* have used to describe the naturally occurring patterns in social behaviors of wolves so that we may better study and catalog them.

Since rank is, fundamentally, mostly about reproductive rights, the alpha animals are generally the only animals with sufficient social freedom to both mate and successfully rear young. Males tend to seek rank primarily over other males and females tend to seek rank primarily over other females (Schenkel, 1947; Haber, 1977). This does not mean that males and females do not dominate each other, but rank differences between a male and a female wolf tend not to be as pronounced as those between wolves of the same gender, and may even appear to be unrelated to their relationships with same-gender wolves (a high ranking female may submit to or court a lower ranking male, for example).

Very young puppies (birth to twelve weeks) have a "rank order," of a sort, among themselves but this is exceptionally informal and may change daily, or even hourly, and be abruptly reversed as the pups play, organize themselves, and grow. "Rank" does not really seem to apply to puppies, who are afforded the privileges of the young, and are often allowed to eat before the adults and to retain pieces of food in their possession even when confronted with a higher ranking adult wolf. "Puppy privileges" begin to diminish as early as six months of age, and wear off at approximately one to two years, when the pups reach puberty. At about the same time, they will likely be considering a move to an adjacent pack or striking off on their own to form a new pack, in which they will automatically be high ranking by dint of being a founding member.

The relative rank of some individuals can be spotted even in wild packs simply by observing and measuring who is submitting to whom. These individuals tend to stick out in the minds of researchers simply because they are so easily identified. However, these eye-catching characteristics do not imply that the individual animal is any more or less important *to the other wolves* than any other wolf. These individuals simply tend to capture the mind of humans, who can get a little fanciful in describing them.

In any given group, there is an animal which is lower in rank than any other animal in that group. It can be easily identified because no other wolf ever submits to it. This animal is often referred to as the "omega" wolf. It may be male or female, and its position may be essentially benign, especially in a laid back pack with a stable rank order. It may simply be the wolf to whom no one submits, with no other special attention paid it. It may alternatively, especially in captivity, be a "scapegoat" animal, the target of the other wolves' pent-up frustrations or aggression due to their lack of opportunity for output elsewhere. The omega position is less pronounced in wild packs. In the wild, a badly treated low ranking wolf usually opts to simply leave the pack. In captivity, it may hang around in its low status for months or years, or may even need to be removed from the enclosure for its own safety. A low ranking wolf often attempts to diffuse potentially aggressive approaches by higher ranking wolves by enticing them into play behaviors instead of dominance behaviors. Also, a low ranking wolf often gets along better with young puppies, who are not yet focused on rank order, than with higher ranking wolves. In this way, the omega position has become associated, in some circles, with some sort of mystical "jester" position which encourages play among the pack or guards the puppies from harm. The omega may well fulfill these roles, but there is no "charter" that says the omega is "supposed" to perform these acts, and some omegas may never perform them.

A lower-ranking wolf "gives paw" to a higher ranking one. Note the relatively calm demeanor of both animals. Photo courtesy of Monty Sloan.

Likewise, the alpha pair—easily identifiable in field research because they submit to no one—do not necessarily "lead" or otherwise give deliberate instruction to the group. As the animals with the most social freedom, the alpha pair are more likely to initiate hunting, group greeting, or traveling behavior, but any wolf in the pack can initiate a group behavior. The alpha pair is not necessarily the first to eat—whichever wolf happens to be holding a piece of food generally gets to keep possession of it no matter who asks for it. Nor are the alphas always the only ones to reproduce. Especially in a large pack, more than one pair may mate and more than one female may give birth. The alpha pair, simply put, is *usually* the only pair to breed, and *usually* the only pair of wolves in the pack with sufficient social freedom and resources to successfully raise pups. There is no evidence that the alphas give "orders" to lower ranking wolves or that there are any specific roles that they play. Simply by dint of being the animals with the most social freedom (because they have no higher ranking animals to whom they submit), they tend to be the first to initiate behaviors and are the ones most likely to have other wolves follow their example.

Because higher rank translates to a greater amount of social freedom (especially the freedom to reproduce), animals which actively strive for higher rank tend to be better represented in the population than animals which do not. Thus, a wolf's drive for rank is inbuilt genetically and is very powerful. Debatably, it starts as soon as the pups are born, when they begin to wrestle and test each other's strengths and weaknesses. As juveniles, they engage in "play" fights and mock aggression, which gives them some idea of the "rules" of engagement and how far they can go before the other animal retaliates. Through this mock aggression, a sort of proto-rank order sets in, and they learn both how to appease higher ranking animals and how to elicit appeasement from lower ranking animals as their own relative rank changes. As adults, they spend much of their free time carefully watching other pack members, looking for opportunities to rise in rank, and making sure others do not rise in rank at their expense.

A higher ranking wolf expresses his status with only a look. Photo courtesy of Monty Sloan.

Striving for rank order does not always mean a huge, damaging fight. Lower-ranking wolves watch higher ranking pack members as they might watch prey, looking for weaknesses or openings into which they might fit themselves with minimal risk. They poke and prod and stretch boundaries, seeing how far they can push the higher ranking wolf before getting told off for their importunity. Then they do it again. And again. And again. This behavior is commonly known as "testing," and can range from merely playing mild games such as "Can You Feel It When I Do This?" to trying to knock the target over under the guise of an over-exuberant greeting behavior, to outright attack, and attempts to intimidate should the target be caught in a compromising position. This social testing can be mistaken for play because sometimes it stays at that level and never goes further, but benign greeting and apparent play behavior can suddenly turn into dominance testing or an all-out attack should an aspiring wolf find a higher ranking animal in an unfortunate place. Wolves are *always* watching, always looking for an opportunity to become higher ranking, and are always ready to jump if they see a chance to better their social position.

A captive wolf raised to view humans as part of its social group does not always differentiate between its human and wolf pack members when it comes to who is involved in struggles for rank order. Generally, wolf pups automatically treat adult humans (if they have contact with them) as dominant, just as they would treat their own parents and other adult pack members. When they reach reproductive maturity, however, at approximately two years of age (Seal et al., 1987), they suddenly have a drive to disperse, form their own pack, and become higher ranking. They do not have any innate belief that the human in a human/wolf social relationship should automatically be the higher ranking animal, especially after the wolf reaches puberty. They begin watching their higher ranking pack members—wolf or human—for signs of the opportune moment to rise in rank, and will use any such moments which come their way to their best advantage. Once reaching the age of puberty, a wolf who has lived harmoniously with humans its whole life may "suddenly" begin testing its human pack mates, or even openly challenging them for rank. This does not make the wolf vicious or "mean"—this is *normal wolf behavior* which has been under strong, positive selection pressure for thousands of years. Wolves take opportunities to rise in rank whenever they occur, and do not necessarily differentiate between wolf and human "targets."

This change in attitudes toward humans is the source of the myth that wolves and wolf hybrids are "unpredictable" and will "turn on you" after coexisting apparently peacefully for some time. They are perfectly predictable in this regard. At approximately two years of age, they *become adult wolves* with all the behaviors appropriate thereto, including the "sudden" and "unexpected" desire to rise in rank, which involves testing, challenging, and occasionally attacking higher ranking pack members, wolf or human, in pursuit of their goal.

Not *all* wolves immediately start driving for higher rank at the age of two, of course. Some don't catch on until later, some start earlier, some have a more focused drive, and some less. Some precocious young wolves reach puberty at the age of ten months, and may start their focused testing then. Some captive wolves may never challenge their owners. Some only challenge if an "opportune moment" presents itself, or when forced into a corner, or when they are unfortunately distracted while aggressively aroused at another target. The drive for rank varies enormously, and it is a massively complex thing, but in general it is more pronounced, and a larger part of the animal's life, in wolves than in dogs.

Prey drive in wolves

Pretty much any wild animal's primary, immediate, number one goal is to locate and stuff its face full of food (and, to a lesser extent, water). This drive is a deep-seated, instinctual one, a very basic need, and neonates of all species come into the world already primed for this vital search, with no training necessary. Young birds arrive ready to open their mouths and beg, foals and fawns rise within minutes and move straight for their mother's teat, and even the wriggling, bean-bag-shaped young of wolves and dogs crawl, eyes closed, toward the smell of their mother and search enthusiastically for milk.

When animals get older, the exact nature of the food drive changes, but most are always hungry and always hoping to eat. As active hunters and opportunistic scavengers, wolves are exceptionally enthusiastic on this point. Their default state is to spend a great deal of time looking for small food items, such as rabbits, voles, or rats and, whenever the opportunity arises, to chase down and catch a large animal such as an elk which may be displaying some weakness (a limp or other debilitation) which makes it easy prey. They are always, *always* on the lookout for food, and for things which may become food. Wolves are designed to spend hours every day searching for it, because in the wild food does not arrive twice a day in a large metal bowl. In fact, one of the leading causes of death in wild wolves is starvation (Mech 1972, 1977). The animals who spend every available waking moment trying to obtain food generally eat better than the animals who sit under a log waiting passively for food to arrive. Animals who have eaten more are in better condition and are more likely to be able to reproduce.

The classic "mouse pounce" of a wolf hunting small prey in tall grass. Photo courtesy of Monty Sloan.

The wild wolf's background produces animals who look for food in everything. This makes them potentially very destructive if kept in a human environment. They will tear apart couches to see if the squeaking spring is really a mouse, dig through floors trying to find out if the downstairs neighbors have anything interesting, and tear through walls trying to get at birds and other small animals or simply to see if there is any food outside the house. Their drive to find food is powered by a lot of energy, and they do not come with any pre-installed understanding that kitchen cabinets, rugs, walls, upholstery, or fine china have any intrinsic value. That kind of information needs to be transmitted to them through training and, although training can be effective, it takes a lot of time, reinforcement, alternative input, and redirection to properly channel the massive amounts of energy a wolf puts into locating and obtaining food into more constructive enterprises.

The primary unsuitability of this strong food-seeking drive as it relates to the human home comes in the appetite of the wolf for potentially viewing anything as food until given evidence to the contrary. This serves the opportunistic wolf well in the wild as it is willing to try eating a variety of objects, allowing it to survive on other foodstuffs when its primary prey is not available. Not only does the wolf view stationary objects (deli meat, apples, old newspapers) as potential food, it views objects in motion (pets such as hamsters, birds, cats, or even small dogs) as potential food as well.

In fact, objects in motion can be even more enticing than stationary ones. In the wild, one of the wolf's sources of food is any small, wriggly animal. A wolf is fundamentally keyed in to tiny, darting movements such as those exhibited by cats and small dogs, and does not necessarily have any instinctual discrimination between these animals and the wild rabbits and rats it would chase in nature. The powerful drive to locate and consume food which served its ancestors so well in the wild does not simply go away when the animal is moved into a human home. It continues to function, to the detriment of any small animals with which it may be sharing the home.

The category of "small animal" can, and does, unfortunately, include human children (Raipurohit, 1999). There have been numerous newspaper and magazine articles referencing children being killed by "pet" wolves or hybrids. This is more likely to be a behavior seen in captive wolves who have lost the natural fear of humans which inhibits predatory behavior toward humans in their wild relatives. Wild wolves are usually far too scared of people to have any desire to hunt them for food. In any case, however, no natural inhibition exists in any wolf (wild or captive) to tell it that a human child is somehow "off-limits" as a potential prey item. Human children, especially infants, differ so radically in size, shape, smell, and behavior from human adults that wolves may not even recognize them to be the same species, and certainly have no instinctual basis for generalizing that human infants are to be afforded any special status afforded human adults. Human children, especially very small ones, exhibit uncoordinated movement and high-pitched vocalizations which resemble with uncanny accuracy the movements of wounded small prey in the wild. They can make an attractive target for an animal which is deeply, fundamentally tuned in to locating the presence of such easy food sources and taking advantage of them.

The facial expression of a hunting wolf. Note the lack of apparent concern from the much larger bison. Photo courtesy of Monty Sloan.

This hunting behavior can be mistaken for excited interest and/or affection, because the natural expression of a hunting wolf is open and interested, and does not always suggest predatory arousal to people unfamiliar with natural hunting behavior (who instead are on the lookout for growls and snarls). People often expect hunting wolves to show signs of aggression, like they sometimes do in documentaries, and assume an animal is "good" with children because it shows only an expression of intense interest when exposed to them. This can result in erroneous reports of wolves or hybrids being "good" with children when their behavior is described by someone who does not recognize what is actually predatory stalking.

It should be noted that some rare individual wolves have been known to view, and treat, human children as puppies, offering them parental care. However, this is an *unusual* behavior on the part of the wolf, and the animal's mind can be easily changed through experiences with children who behave more like food than like wolf infants. Wolf Park had a couple of adult wolves who treated children like puppies for years, approaching with friendly and submissive greeting behaviors. At the age of approximately five years, one of the wolves observed, on separate days, two different children throwing temper tantrums in which the children lay on the ground, screamed, and flailed with their fists and legs, resembling wounded prey in no small way. After these incidents, that wolf began showing predatory interest in human children. The other wolf, having never observed a temper tantrum of that sort, lived her whole life treating children as puppies, but she was an exceptional individual and there was still *no guarantee* that a similar experience with a screaming child would not also have changed her mind. In any case, it should be noted that these animals were *never* allowed access to human children while not actively controlled (leashed) by an adult and, of course, the wolf which turned predatory was never again allowed to be on the same side of a fence as a child once the predatory behavior manifested.

The drive for resources/territory in wolves

A wild wolf's life depends on being able to obtain resources—food, shelter, a mate—and then defend these resources from other animals who also wish to possess them. Being well fed and having high social rank avail a wolf nothing if it simply gives up anything it obtains to any wolf that happens to come along. It must have a drive to protect its hard-won resources from other comers, and one way is to defend a territory.

In a wolf pack, even the high-priority activity of achieving a high rank often (but not always) takes a back seat to ownership of a particular, valued object. If an animal is holding an object, sitting on an object, or even if the animal is simply very near an object, that object is "considered" by other wolves to belong to that animal, regardless of rank. Lower ranking animals may "ask," submissively, to be allowed to share the resource, and higher ranking animals may offer threatening gestures in hope of encouraging the other animal to leave voluntarily. But, if a wolf possesses a resource, there is no rule which says it has to give it up without a fight, no matter its rank. Wolves exhibit altruistic behavior from time to time, but no rule in wolf society says, "If someone asks for your toy, you should give it to them." Even very young puppies have a basic sense of the concept of "mine" and "yours," as generations of Wolf Park's "puppy mothers" will tell you.

The wolf on the left "asks" to share a gourd with the wolf on the right. Photo courtesy of Monty Sloan.

This concept of "ownership" and defense of that ownership lands wolves in trouble with humans in more ways than one. The most obvious situation is food-guarding, because food is a resource of primary importance and one of the things that wolves work very hard to procure—and to defend once they have procured it. A wolf who does not acquire any food it can, eat as much of that food as it can very rapidly, and defend it if possible, will not eat well, and hungry wolves are not likely to successfully reproduce. Captive wolves may be so focused on guarding food that they will begin guarding food they have not yet been given. This leads to trouble as a human may still be holding the food the wolf now considers to be its property.

Wolves guard resources, such as toys, mates, food caches, and sometimes favored sleeping spots, with the same enthusiasm with which they defend their food. "Toys," in particular, tend to be highly problematic, since wolves do not discriminate between "toys" such as rawhides, squeaky toys, and bones and "toys" such as shoes, bedding, and the television remote control. Trying to take a "toy" of any sort away from a wolf is an exercise in futility—again, there is no rule in wolf society that a wolf must cede an object to any pack member, not even a dominant one. Careful training can result in a wolf who is willing to *trade* one toy for another, or drop a toy for a valuable treat. However, trying to remove something precious, such as a Christmas roast, hat, or wallet, directly from a wolf's mouth is asking to lose fingers. Again, this is *not "bad" behavior,* and a wolf who bites while defending something it feels that it "owns" is not vicious. The guarding of territory, including items, is *natural wolf behavior* which has been actively selected for over many generations in the wild.

A corollary of territorial behavior is scent marking. Wolves cannot label their possessions with handy little stickers or by writing their names on them in pen. They must label their items with smell, and they have a handy source of some very strong smell easily available and always ready for use. They never run out of "ink" with this handy tool, and will not hesitate to use it to mark both areas and items with their *nom de plume.* This behavior is not linked to a need to eliminate nor can it be corrected by housetraining. Many dogs may also exhibit this behavior. However, scent marking behavior is primarily the realm of *dominant* animals, and most dogs have less desire to be dominant than do most wolves. Also, most dogs are more likely to respond to human training about not eliminating inside the house than are wolves. Dogs can be trained not to scent-mark, especially inside the human home. Wolves generally do not understand the idea of not marking—especially in one's own home, which is what, in a wolf's opinion, most needs to be marked.

My pumpkin. Photo courtesy of Monty Sloan.

Wolves have no inbuilt information about human society. They do not automatically know that your wallet is more important than their favorite chewy toy, or that it belongs to you. If you aren't holding it, after all, it is fair game. Likewise, they do not come with a belief that one "should" eliminate only outdoors. In the wild, there is no place that one does not eliminate. Everything wolves know about human society must be taught to them as they grow—and, even if taught appropriate rules, they have no inbuilt motivation to listen to anything humans say. Again, this is not malicious or rebellious behavior on the part of the wolf—this is *normal wolf behavior*. Their goal is to eat a lot, be the highest ranking animal around, and to possess anything and everything that takes their fancy. Wolves who accomplish these goals in the wild are most likely to reproduce, and their genes are most likely to be represented in future generations.

Behavioral characteristics of the dog

Dog behavior is still based, to varying degrees, on the basic original template of wolf behavior, but that template has been modified in all sorts of ways by selective breeding. Human interaction with and alteration of dogs has created the wide variety of behavior patterns we now see but some general tendencies are clear. Dogs do not generally exhibit as strong a desire for high rank as do wolves, at least where it concerns challenging humans for rank. People have tended to not breed animals who challenge them in that way. Dogs bark more than wolves, possibly because in some situations humans have found that behavior to be beneficial. Predatory aggression (the tendency to hunt) has also been in many cases significantly reduced. Dogs do not need to chase or catch food since it is provided to them by humans. Greeting and submissive behaviors such as licking, tail wagging, and begging have increased in frequency relative to wolves, since humans tend to like those behaviors. Aggressive behaviors in most cases have decreased, since humans tend not to feed or protect dogs who are aggressive toward them or toward their other pets. Of course, humans have also bred some dogs specifically for their aggressive tendencies or guarding abilities. Examples include Dobermans and Rottweilers for their guarding abilities, and certain Hounds and many Terriers for their predatory behaviors.

It is difficult to put absolutes on dog behavior—variation is so great that, for any given behavior, one is guaranteed to find at least one dog who exhibits it, as well as one who does not. However, a good rule is that dogs display behavior which generally makes them "good with people" (Fox, 1978). This includes a lower drive for predatory behavior, a lower drive for rank (which includes increased display of submissive behaviors), and a lower drive for territorial defense (of food, territory, and mates). One will find exceptions, of course, but *compared to wolves,* dogs are almost always on the "good with people" end of the spectrum in these behavior traits. We will examine this in Chapter 3.

Prey drive in dogs

Dogs, after thousands of years of selective breeding, still have a lot of the wolf's original prey drive, but it has been put through the funhouse mirror of domestication. Most dogs are always hungry, but in general dogs do not expend the same kind of energy on locating food, nor do they have the same single minded drive that powers the wolf into taking apart kitchens, garages, and appliances in attempting to locate food or replicate the sensory input of the hunt. While many dogs do have the basic desire to chase prey (cars, squirrels, cats), the behavior pattern, altered significantly by domestication, often naturally "derails" around, or even before, the time the dog catches the object. The dog has not had to hunt regularly for its food in many generations and may not know what to do with its freshly caught prey, and will either play with it or let it go. The dog may exhibit good hunting behavior, but be too small (for example, a Chihuahua) to do any damage to its intended prey. The dog is also much more likely than a wolf to listen to communications from its owner ("No!" or "Come!") concerning its choice of target, and much more likely to regard humans he knows as dominant enough to have their orders be worth following.

A Border Collie "hunts" the moving end of a rake. Photo courtesy of Monty Sloan.

Certainly there are dogs that single-mindedly pursue, catch, and kill chickens and cats. In some cases, selective breeding has been used to enhance, alter, or modify the predatory extinct, especially in the breeds we use to hunt or herd. Picture Border Collies herding sheep, a wonderful example of modified and enhanced predatory behavior, or Greyhounds and Borzois running down prey such as jackrabbits for a rancher who may want to eliminate them. However, there are *many* more safeguards with dogs compared to wolves in that their efforts may derail, or be ineffective, and/or can be interrupted successfully by human intervention or by preventative training.

While dogs are also certainly capable of viewing very young humans as prey, and many unfortunate accounts exist of dogs mauling human infants because they mistake them for prey items, dogs have undergone thousands of years of careful breeding to insure that they are more likely to view humans as members of their pack, and usually the dominant ones. With dogs, infant humans are much more likely to be given the same exalted status as their human parents, and be treated as puppies rather than prey, exempt to the rule of "if it wiggles, bite it" that so many wolves follow naturally. Dogs have been selectively bred for many, many generations to achieve even this often-disturbed delicate balance. Wolves have *no history whatsoever* which tells them that human infants are not food. This has often been used as an argument for judging wolves as good or evil, as discussed elsewhere in the book. It is neither. Biting is simply what they have been programmed by their environment to do. In any event, both dogs and wolves are capable of injuring or killing people.

Drive for rank and resources in dogs

The drive for rank in dogs has had an especially exciting ride through the process of domestication (Wickens and Bradshaw, 1993). Humans usually have no interest whatsoever in breeding animals which attack higher ranking pack members—especially human ones. Why would you want *copies* of something that attacked you when it hit sexual maturity? Dogs have been under strong selection pressure for many, many generations to not consider gaining rank a high priority. Also, various side effects of domestication—discussed later in this book—have helped to aid the human desire to have "rank-free" dogs. Dogs generally never "grow up" and develop the full adult wolf drive for higher rank. In contrast to the wolf, they do not need to depend on higher social rank in order to successfully obtain food and reproduce. Thus, they tend to lose interest, over the generations, in expending valuable energy on obtaining a social status which confers no benefit.

Especially in dogs, tug-of-war is usually more game than territorial expression. Photo courtesy of Monty Sloan.

Of course, dogs still have social hierarchies (Cafazzo et al., 2008), and some dogs do attempt to achieve higher rank over humans. This is the exception to the rule, however, and dogs are *much* less likely to challenge their human pack members for dominance, or to exhibit the same amount of dedication in their efforts, as do wolves. Dogs may defend food, toys and other resources to varying degrees (Cafazzo et al.,

2008), but generally not with the same zeal as do wolves (Fox, 1978). Humans are not generally interested in feeding animals which bite them as they put down the food bowl, or which have to be pinned in a corner and held down in order to retrieve valuable items from them. Thousands of years of selective breeding have produced animals whose natural tendency to guard has been altered or derailed at the instinctive level by the process of evolution itself, and may simply cede favored resources to those higher ranking humans when asked in order to avoid confrontation. Some dogs simply have no instinctual guarding behavior, having had it bred out of them during domestication.

On the other hand, some dogs are notorious resource guarders. Ironically, it may be that a person has inadvertently reinforced guarding behavior if, for example, the dog finds that growling at the person reaching for a favorite toy "works." Alternatively, they may have some instinctual guarding behavior, but require immensely powerful stimuli (a female in estrous, a gravy-dipped steak currently in their mouth) to elicit it. Some will never display guarding behavior over low quality items such as mere dry dog food, children's toys, or used tissue. Other dogs, having no desire to rise in rank, simply regard humans as dominant their whole lives, and simply automatically cede valuable items to the dominant humans when asked. As with wolves, rank and resource guarding seen in dogs varies significantly.

Your mileage may vary

We are certain that some of our readers have encountered in the previous paragraphs points with which they may disagree. We pause here to emphasize that *with animals, there are no absolutes.* We are certain that some of our readers know, or may even own, a wolf who, for example, loves to be a "couch potato" and has never been interested in social rank or challenging humans, a wolf who is good with children, a wolf who regularly cedes her dinner to anyone who asks, or a wolf who makes a perfect pet. And some people have undoubtedly owned a dog who behaves like a wolf. We have to emphasize, however, that these animals are *the exception* to general rules we have seen in our years of experience with wolves and dogs. We like to say that with any given individual wolf or dog, "your mileage may vary."

Wolf Park's well-behaved, socialized wolves howl companionably along with a keeper. Not all wolf-human relationships are this peaceful. Photo courtesy of Monty Sloan.

Most of our experience with "non-template" animals was at Wolf Park. There we encountered a few wolves who, in some fashion, did not quite match the general standard. The Park has been home to a couple of wolves who did not quite master the concept of "rank order" until their third or fourth birthdays, or even at all. The Park has met wolves who were wonderful with human children, treating them as puppies (at least until the children gave them reason to think otherwise). Many of Wolf Park's animals, because of intensive, careful and thorough training, are happy to trade one precious item (a cell phone) for another precious item (a used tissue) upon polite request, although their natural inclination is to guard their new, valuable possession, not to trade it. These animals do exist. However, they are the exceptions. The vast majority of the wolves the Park has encountered have been very interested—*especially compared to dogs*—in food, in rank order, and in territory, to the point where they would be unsuccessful trying to live peacefully in an average human home.

Likewise, there are definitely some humans out there who are well prepared to deal with animals who have high drives for prey, territory, and rank, and who would make perfect owners for even the most focused wolf. We cannot deny that these people exist, either. However, these people are also the exception as most people are not ready to deal with that kind of behavior, or at least are not looking for that kind of behavior in a potential household pet.

Knowing that this book will be read not just by rescues and shelters, but also by people curious about wolves and hybrids and perhaps interested in obtaining one as a pet, we must emphasize that, in our experience, not many people are prepared, either financially or mentally, to own an animal which exhibits a high degree of wild type wolf behavior. This is part of the reason so many people are concerned about wolf percentages in their pets, or in their clients' pets. While there are certainly some mellow, dog-like wolves out there, no one can guarantee that any individual animal you may encounter will be in that lucky, exceptional minority. We cannot in good conscience encourage the general public to rush out and purchase pet wolves by making statements like "wolves can be good with children" and "not all wolves are interested in rank." The most likely scenario, with any given random wolf, is that it will be one of the majority of wolves that think human children and small pets are prey items, are interested in increasing their social rank and defending their territory, and that generally do not behave like a domestic dog. One will find exceptions to every rule, but the emphasis in this book must remain upon the rules themselves.

CHAPTER 3
Domestication: From Wolf to Dog

So now we have the "wolf" and the "dog," two kinds of animal which have some behavioral and physical similarities and distinctions from one another, and the notion that a process occurred which made some of the one (the "wolf") change into the other (the "dog").

The nature of this process is complicated and, so far, incompletely understood. Until now, we have talked about the wolf and the dog as two "species," implying that each is a separate group of animals, with separate looks and behavior, with not a lot of meeting in the middle. In real life the line between "wolf" and "dog" is very blurry, and it starts blurring even at the most basic level. Even declaring them separate species has been a debatable point since the Smithsonian's 1993 reclassification of the dog as a subspecies (a subset, if you will, of a species—a population genetically distinguishable from other populations of the same species yet capable of interbreeding successfully with them) of wolf. In this chapter we will explore both the wolf and the dog, and how—and if—one should differentiate between the two, and how that mysterious process may have occurred wherein the one might have come from the other.

The origin of "species"

"I was much struck by how entirely vague and arbitrary is the distinction between species and varieties." ~ Charles Darwin

Humans have been arguing about the definition of the word "species" almost since we began naming animals. The "science" of scientific nomenclature began with Linnaeus, whose *Systema Naturae* (1735) is generally considered to be the beginning of formal taxonomy. Unfortunately, quite a lot of the world had not yet been fully explored when he wrote his book, and Linnaeus was unaware of things like DNA. As we learn more about the world, we find that "species" becomes harder and harder to define.

It is likely we can all agree that the elephant and the hippopotamus, for example, are two different species—they look very different, live in different habitats, and do not interbreed. So what about the Baltimore oriole (*Icterus galbula*) and the Bullock's oriole (*Icterus bullockii*), two small, black and yellow colored birds extremely similar in size, feeding habits, and habitat?

Baltimore Oriole. Photo courtesy of David Brezinski, USFWS.

Bullock's Oriole. Photo courtesy of Kevin Cole, through Flickr Creative Commons.

These two species of birds have overlapping ranges and can produce fertile offspring. In fact, they were once considered the same species, the "Northern oriole," until DNA studies proved that they were not as closely related as appearance, behavior, and location would indicate. To confuse matters further, the two species were called "orioles" by settlers arriving in America because they looked like European orioles, but in fact are not related to the true orioles, which are in the family Oriolidae.

The debate about how to delineate species continues as DNA analysis has become more sophisticated and more detailed comparisons of populations can be conducted. Wolves and dogs have been shown, through such analysis, to share approximately 99% of their DNA (Wayne and Ostlander, 1999). They are even more closely related than the two nearly identical little birds pictured above. As one can probably guess, the definition of "species" gets a little stretched when talking about dogs and wolves.

The original working definition of "species," in fact, was "a population of similar individuals who breed readily with each other and cannot interbreed with other populations," with speciation being defined by the arising of barriers to interbreeding (Arnold, 1997). Since dogs and wolves readily produce offspring together, they would *not* be considered different species under this definition. A clearer definition of species, currently in use, is "a visually and behaviorally distinct population of animals which, because of geographical location, or behavioral or physiological differences, *rarely* hybridizes with other populations." Dogs and wolves, left to their own devices, interbreed infrequently, generally because of differences in behavior and habitat (Vilà and Wayne, 1999). Under this definition, they could well be considered separate species.

The classification of animals into species changes over time as opinions come and go, but seems to be less about categorization of animals according to differences and similarities and more a function of semantics and/or politics. For years, because of differences in behavior and habitat between the two, scientists considered wolves and dogs to be two species: *Canis lupus*, the wolf, and *Canis familiaris*, the dog. It was only relatively recently (1993) that a major scientific publication—the Smithsonian Institution's *Mammal Species of the World*—redefined the dog as a subspecies of wolf, labeling it *Canis lupus familiaris*. Wolves and dogs didn't change, but our opinion of them did. Of course, that is not the end of the argument. The debate over their exact classification may continue indefinitely. Recent DNA investigations imply that not only do wolf hybrids crop up in captivity, they also crop up in the wild—wolves and dogs (and coyotes, and jackals, and dingoes, and...) have, it seems, been interbreeding, infrequently but consistently, for generations, thus muddying the definition of "wolf" and "dog" still further (Coppinger, 2009; Kyle et al., 2008, 2006; Pilgrim et al., 1998; Tsuda et al., 1997; Vilà and Wayne, 1997; Lehman et al., 1991; and a host of others). There are "pure wolves" in the wild who have both coyote and dog DNA (Aldhous, 2008). Just as likely, there are "pure dogs" who have both coyote and wolf DNA. How are we to tell them apart? *Can* we distinguish between wolves and dogs?

Dr. Raymond Coppinger, in a paper which began as a semi-facetious after dinner speech entitled "What, if Anything, is a Wolf?" points out the flaws in our system of nomenclature. He describes how the "species" we call dogs, wolves, coyotes, jackals, etc., are really a single population of animals varying in size and shape depending on their habitat, and uses semantics to humorously prove that all canids are the same species. By this logic the wolf is, in fact, a subspecies of dog. The publication-ready version of that speech (Coppinger, 2009), much altered and now complete with some pretty convincing computer simulations, demonstrates that current DNA analysis may need some serious rethinking before it will be ready to paint an accurate picture of genealogical timelines. Coppinger presents the theory that *all* canids, not just domestic dogs and gray wolves, are the same species—simply part of a huge "cline," or gradation, of morphs of one species whose population spans almost the whole of the globe.

That conclusion may not be as far from the truth as it may seem. We simply do not currently have enough information about how groups of animals grow, move, change, and interact with each other to definitively tell "wolf" apart from "dog"—or even to decide if there is an "apart" to be told. From the definition of "species" to the definition of "wolf" and "dog," science has yet to come to a formal conclusion. As DNA analysis techniques improve and we discover more about the interrelationships of species, we may yet unearth even more bizarre concepts to further complicate our already obfuscated picture of wolves, dogs, and hybrids.

Fortunately for the layman, it does not matter, in a practical sense, whether scientists consider the wolf and the dog to be two species or one. What scientists would call any individual animal is rarely relevant in a chance encounter or a rescue situation. The point of the matter is that the wolf and the dog are very closely related while being at the same time distinct enough that we have a natural inclination, by dint of having detected some obvious differences between them, to try to tell them apart.

While scientific debates about the definition of "species," "wolf," and "dog" will no doubt continue, the dog appears to be best mentally pictured, for the moment at least, as a subspecies of wolf. This particular subspecies likely descended from one or more select lines of wolves who learned it might be advantageous to utilize the resource of human garbage and, in doing so, changed the selection pressures active upon themselves.

Evolution in a nutshell

> *"Most species do their own evolving, making it up as they go along, which is the way Nature intended. And this is all very natural and organic and in tune with mysterious cycles of the cosmos, which believes that there's nothing like millions of years of really frustrating trial and error to give a species moral fiber and, in some cases, backbone." ~ Terry Pratchett*

In a population of animals, a variety of environmental pressures affect how likely any individual animal is to be able to survive and reproduce. For example, in an area with high ambient temperatures, animals which are better able to withstand high temperatures are going to be less stressed than animals which cannot withstand them. Animals which are less stressed by the heat are more likely to successfully reproduce, so they will produce more offspring than animals which are more stressed by the heat. These offspring will be, like their parents, more able to deal with hot weather. Eventually, most of the population of animals will consist of individuals who are not stressed by heat, simply because the un-stressed animals have produced so many more offspring that they have simply outnumbered, or *outcompeted*, the stressed animals. This is, put very simply, the process of evolution.

The classic example of evolution at work involves the tale of the peppered moth (*Biston betularia*). A native of England, the moths were originally a beautiful light gray color, with soft brown spots. This camouflaged them well against the light colored trees and rocks in their habitat. The Industrial Revolution, early in the nineteenth century, brought about great changes in the English countryside in which peppered moths lived, including deposits of soot which formed on trees and rocks, darkening the surfaces on which the moths rested. In 1848, a dark colored, or *melanistic*, peppered moth was identified—likely the result of a spontaneous mutation. The dark moth was very well camouflaged when it landed on the sooty rocks and trees compared to the original light gray moth which now stood out prominently against soot and were easy targets for birds and other predators. This made the dark moths less likely to be eaten by predators and therefore more likely than light moths to survive and to reproduce. By 1895, more than 90% of peppered moths in England were melanistic (Steward, 1977). In fact, over 70 different species of moths in England underwent a transformation from light to dark. Species in other countries have undergone similar changes as well. Today, as environmental cleanliness standards rise, the countryside of England is becoming cleaner again, with less soot, and the original, light-colored moths are once again becoming more prevalent.

Though the changes in the peppered moth came about within a hundred year period, evolutionary change generally occurs much more slowly. It usually takes hundreds of generations, and thousands of years, for significant change to occur. A recent experiment demonstrated the scope of this process by raising *Escherichia coli* bacteria on a medium which contained citrate. Normal *E. coli* bacteria cannot use citrate for much of anything. After thirty thousand generations of bacteria, however, the normal process of random genetic mutation produced a single mutant strain of E. coli which could process citrate (Blount et al., 2008). Thirty thousand generations is a long time, even in bacteria! It would take thirty thousand *years* in a species which, like wolves, produces one litter a year. (Actually, it would likely take even longer than that, as female wolves do not usually produce a litter until their second year.)

A dog is born: Domesticating the wolf

"He is your friend, your partner, your defender, your dog. You are his life, his love, his leader. He will be yours, faithful and true, to the last beat of his heart. You owe it to him to be worthy of such devotion." ~ Unknown

Evolution is the process by which animals change to adapt to the pressures of their environment. *Domestication*, the process by which a select group of wolves likely became dogs, is a highly focused occurrence of evolution, helped along by man being beneficial or detrimental to individual animals based on his own personal preferences. Man does not even have to partake *consciously* in this process. Animals are affected by the presence and actions of man whether man is directly taking an interest in them or not.

A black Labrador Retriever. Photo courtesy of C J Hughson (60north), through Flickr Creative Commons.

It is generally agreed that the dog was the first animal to be domesticated (Ostrander et al., 2006). Archaeological records show canids with physical distinctions from wolves found in human settlements from fourteen to fifteen thousand years ago (Nobis, 1979; Sablin and Khlopachev, 2002). (The word "canids" is used here to describe the members of the family *Canidae*, which includes both wolves and dogs.)

Originally, humans and wolves left each other pretty much alone. No one is totally certain how or why wolves and humans started living together. However, a very good working theory, and the one to which we ascribe, is outlined in Ray and Lorna Coppinger's excellent book, *Dogs, A New Understanding of Canine Origin, Behavior and Evolution*. The Coppingers assert that wolves and humans started interacting several thousand years or so ago. They believe this started when wolves learned that the garbage that primitive humans were leaving behind as they traveled from camp to camp contained a potentially easy-to-obtain source of food, and started following the humans, and their food, around. This changed the developmental patterns of a certain subgroup of wolves which found it beneficial to live near human garbage dumps. (It seems likely that humans may have also found these wolves to function as early warning systems *vis à vis* other people and predators; thus the benefits may have flowed both ways.)

Wolves who interacted regularly with humans ended up living under very different environmental pressures than did wolves who did not interact with humans. "Living with humans" was an entirely different world, after all, than "living in the wild" (Fox, 1978). Humans provided food, some protection from predators, and perhaps shelter and water. They may also have selectively fed or protected especially useful or beautiful animals, enhancing their chances at reproduction. Under these new selective pressures, the human-tolerant wolves began to change (Frank and Frank, 1982).

Initially at least, these wolves became smaller—there was no use wasting energy on becoming large enough to hunt large game when someone is feeding you. Their brains also got smaller (Coppinger and Schneider, 1995), because you don't need a large brain to catch garbage. Today, the brains of large dogs are about the same size (100cc) as those of four-month-old wolves (Coppinger and Coppinger, 1998). Brains are the most metabolically expensive organ in the body, requiring more than twenty-two times the amount of energy to "run" as does a similarly-sized amount of, say, muscle (Aiello, 1997). There are not many calories in garbage with which to maintain a big brain, and large brains are not necessary in order to "hunt" garbage. There was no point to wasting resources on growing big brains they didn't need.

Their behaviors changed, too. The biggest change was that the wolves who lived near humans became, genetically, less fearful of humans. If there were thirty wolves, for example, feeding off a pile of human garbage near a camp, those thirty wolves would have been competing with each other to see how much food they could eat before the humans chased them away. If a human approached, the most fearful wolves would run first. Once they ran, they no longer had access to the food source. Less fearful wolves would wait until the human got much closer before they turned and ran, obtaining more of the food before they were chased away. The wolves who waited longer to run got more of the food and were better able to raise pups, because they were healthier. Over time, the "calm" wolves raised more pups than the "timid" wolves, and "calm" animals began to predominate in the gene pool. (There was a downside to being less fearful, of course. The most fearless wolves may have walked right into the village, where they were likely seen as a threat and killed—also a bad choice from a reproductive standpoint. Likely, the wolves who survived to reproduce were at a "happy medium" point between fearless and fearful.)

It seems then that two processes were likely involved in the domestication of the wolf somewhat simultaneously. The first process involved the wolves who were finding it beneficial to scavenge near humans. In essence, these wolves were starting a selective breeding program among themselves, "selecting," though certainly neither consciously nor deliberately, for a tolerance of human presence. The more tolerant wolves got more time at the food source and thus more resources. This pressure, selecting only for tolerance of human presence, changed the degree of human-tolerance expressed by the wolves over generations.

What is fascinating about the change in the genetically-coded preference for human tolerance is that it also affected the expression of other genes. Research conducted on silver foxes (Trut, 1999; Belyaev, 1969) found that the trait "tolerance of humans" is at least partly based on the production of corticosteroids. The genes in silver foxes (and wolves and dogs) which code for production of corticosteroids are *linked* to a number of other genes. When the corticosteroid genes are altered, the other, linked, genes are altered, too. Changing how tame the animals were by changing how corticosteroids were expressed also created the opportunity for the *incidental* (not deliberately selected for) change in expression of a number of other genes. These other genetic changes, linked to the changes in corticosteroid production, included increased displays of juvenile behavior in adults, multiple breeding seasons instead of just one, white patches in the fur, unusually long fur, underbites and overbites, and curly or shortened tails. Because the genes governing a wolf's tolerance of humans were linked to many other genes, changing the frequency and degree of expression of tolerance changed the frequency and degree of expression of those other, linked genes. As the wolves became more and more genetically human-tolerant, the accidental, but linked, traits like floppy ears, curly tails, and white patches of fur (all of which are seen in many dogs) happened to proliferate alongside the increased manifestation of human tolerance (Wayne, 2001).

Which came first, the tameness or the spots? Photo courtesy of Monty Sloan.

The second process, which probably started about the same time as the first but certainly was not as intense—was selective breeding by humans for specific traits which were useful to them. The wolves, as they unconsciously selected themselves to promote tolerance of humans, likely produced unusual individual wolves which barked a lot, made good guard animals, or were willing to help humans hunt by lending the services of eyes, ears, or nose in exchange for a share of the kill. Some became exceptionally beautifully colored or shaped in ways which humans found attractive. Once the usefulness of these wolves became recognized, people, either indirectly through selectively feeding and protecting these animals, or directly by capturing these animals and deliberately breeding them, began to reap the benefits of offspring displaying the desired traits. This would have encouraged even more selective breeding to increase those traits into the population (Clutton-Brock, 1987). This process was no doubt slow at first, but later became the predominant process in dog domestication. We know that the modern refinement of most dog breeds was brought about by human selective breeding, as AKC records can attest, but the original work was begun almost accidentally, by the wolves themselves and by their new human companions as they learned to live together.

Changes in these wolves, as they became dogs, were generally not the result of the new selective pressures creating *new* genetic material/genes/appearances/traits out of thin air, but of working with *already existing* genetic codes and changing which ones were expressed and how intensely they were expressed (Vilà et al., 1997; Fox, 1978). All behaviors exhibited by the dog are thus based on, or very closely related to, the original wolf behaviors. In fact, much dog behavior very closely resembles the behavior of the juvenile wolf (Coppinger and Schneider, 1995; Frank and Frank, 1982)—which may be why so many people find that very young wolves make relatively decent house pets prior to puberty. All dog behavior is, therefore, essentially wolf behavior, modified to various extents by the dog breed's history of interactions with humans and by the individual animal's immediate bloodlines and upbringing (Kukekova, et al., 2006).

This means that *any* dog, no matter what breed or what size, has the potential to exhibit *any* specific behavior we commonly associate with the wolf. It may be that years of domestication have altered the stimuli which cause those behaviors to manifest, or modified the sequence of displayed behaviors, but all those behaviors are there, and can manifest at any time, given sufficient prodding or the necessary stimuli, in any dog. There are dogs who have "wolfy" color patterns in their coats, there are dogs who are "escape artists," there are dogs who display predatory behavior towards small pets, there are dogs who live in pack situations with wolf-like "ranks," and there are dogs who display territorial or food aggression. There are also dogs who howl. Dr. Erich Klinghammer, who founded Wolf Park, often demonstrated the wolf-like behavior of his "pocket wolves" (pet Chihuahuas) during educational presentations, the miniscule dogs howling enthusiastically along with their more wild-type kin on the other side of the enclosure fence.

Domestication vs. taming

"A wild goose never reared a tame gosling." - Irish proverb

Domestication is a process wherein *generations* of animals become progressively better adapted to living with people through selective breeding. Under this paradigm, animals who coexist well with humans live to reproduce, and they produce offspring who are also well suited to living with humans. Animals who don't work well with humans don't reproduce, and vanish from the gene pool. Domestication is a genetic process, affecting not an individual animal, but a whole population of animals over many generations. Thus, offspring born to a domesticated animal are also domesticated.

Domestication is often confused with taming, a process done to an *individual* animal during its lifetime. Taming is simply a process of reducing the animal's flight distance (the distance at which an animal will flee) from humans to zero. This can be done to any animal, at any age. Wild animals can be tamed. A common image is one of a "wild" squirrel, raccoon, or deer who will willingly approach people for treats. The animals are genetically indistinguishable from their non-tame counterparts, and their offspring will not be born tame. Some domesticated animals are also not tame—for example, some dogs are very shy and will not approach people. These are still domesticated animals descended from generations of domesticated animals. They are simply not tame.

This wolf is tame, not domesticated. Photo by Jessica Addams.

You can take a wild wolf, bring it into a human society, and tame it. It will not run from people and may behave decently in captivity, depending on where it lives and how it is handled. However, it will still be a wolf, not a "domesticated wolf," because its genetic code has not been altered at all by your efforts to reduce it personal flight distance to zero. If that wolf has puppies, they will not be born tame. You will have to tame the puppies as well. However, if you take a *population* of wolves and carefully breed them together, allowing only individuals who enjoy the company of humans to reproduce, eventually you will get a lot of wolves who really enjoy the company of humans. Their offspring, when born, will also enjoy the company of humans. As described earlier, we humans have already performed this process on wolves. The "domesticated wolf" is called the dog.

Common themes in domesticated animals

Wolves are not the only animals which humans have domesticated. Humans have domesticated cattle, sheep, and pigs (picture their wild cousins, the bison, the bighorn sheep, and the boar), as well as goats, horses, chickens, rats, and the domestic cat among many other species.

What the process of domestication does to animals, both intentionally and unintentionally, is a fascinating study. Domesticated animals share a number of characteristics, although each was domesticated separately. A great number of domesticated species, as their expression of "tolerance for humans" increased, also developed spotted pelts (for example, cattle, goats, dogs, cats, and horses), floppy ears (dogs, rabbits), or domed foreheads (some dogs, some cats, Arabian horses). Many also changed so that instead of breeding once a year like their wild cousins, they bred twice (or more) a year, or year round instead of only during one season (dogs, cats, cattle, horses). Remember that these traits are linked to the genes which control tolerance of humans, and that changing the degree of tolerance changes how these linked traits are expressed.

The short, rounded, neotenous muzzle of a Boxer. Photo courtesy of Monty Sloan.

Another common factor in domestication seems to be the preservation of juvenile behaviors, such as food begging and submissive greeting behavior, into adulthood. This occurs alongside the preservation of juvenile physical characteristics, such as the aforementioned domed forehead. When an animal retains juvenile characteristics into adulthood, it is called *neoteny*, or *pedomorphosis*. In a very real sense, the domestication process in wolves produced a strain of neotenous wolves called "dogs," who act (and in some cases look) like juvenile wolves their entire lives (Trut, 2004; Wayne, 2001; Goodwin et al., 1997; Coppinger and Schneider, 1995; Frank and Frank, 1982; Fox, 1978). These "juvenile adult" dogs view humans as higher-ranking parents their whole lives, and generally never mature behaviorally to the point of striking out on their own and starting a new pack, or taking over their current pack (of course, as in all things related to dog behavior, there are exceptions).

I started with a wolf and made this?

"I wonder if other dogs think poodles are members of a weird religious cult."
~ Rita Rudner, comedienne

In his classic *The Dog: Its Domestication and Behavior*, Fox describes how the process of domestication affects behavior in this way: "How an animal behaves is more or less phylogenetically fixed, but when and to whom it behaves as well as the threshold and sequencing of behavioral units is affected by domestication and early experience."

The wolf is the original template for the dog despite how different they may be today. Photos courtesy of Monty Sloan.

This leads to a nice shorthand description of the wolf and the dog. The wolf is the original model, as it were, with all the classic "options." It is still suited for living in the wild, catching its own food, and working appropriately with a pack. The dog is the wolf viewed through a funhouse mirror—still resembling its wild cousin, but with some attributes larger or smaller than normal, some a little oddly shaped, and some missing altogether. The amount of "fun" in the funhouse mirror varies, of course, by the breed of dog (Goodwin et al., 1997).

Further reading on the topic of domestication may be found in the Recommended Reading section at the back of the book.

CHAPTER 4
When Wolves and Dogs Combine: A Genetics Primer

So what really happens when wolves and dogs combine? A lack of common knowledge of genetics as well as a lack of common sense have produced some unusual ideas surrounding wolf and dog genetics. In order to clarify what really goes on when a wolf and dog (or wolf hybrid and wolf hybrid) mate, we must begin even before that beginning, before the egg and sperm meet—when the egg and sperm are being created.

DNA

The cells of every dog and wolf (and animal, and plant) contain a substance called deoxyribonucleic acid, or DNA. DNA is the familiar "double helix" molecule which contains, essentially, the instructions for how to build a wolf or dog at the molecular level. These instructions are encoded in the pattern of the smaller molecules which make up DNA—adenine, thymine, cytosine, and guanine—rather like computer instructions are encoded in the series of ones and zeros called "binary." Nifty little cellular structures "read" the instructions off the strands of DNA, and using those instructions, produce molecules—proteins, hormones, and the like—whose interactions eventually put together an animal.

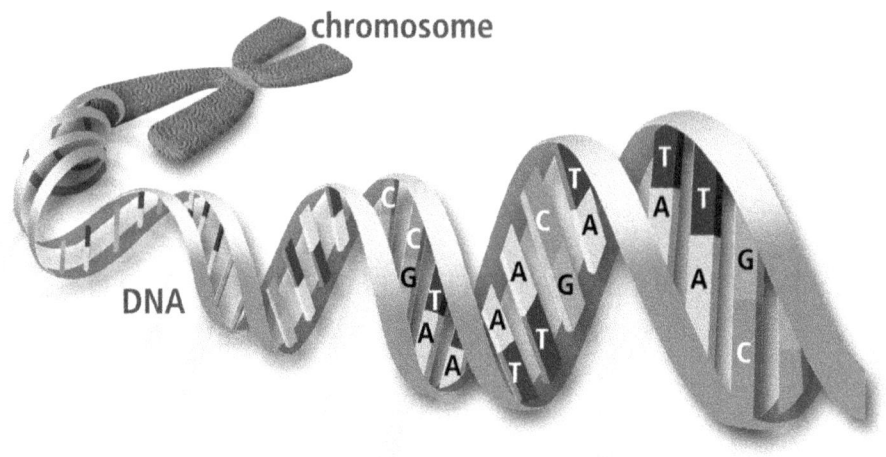

The building blocks which combine to form a living animal are encoded in its DNA. Source: US Dept of Energy: genomics.energy.gov.

A section of DNA which provides instructions for something (the shape of a protein, a hormone, the timing of a growth spurt, etc) is called a gene. Each DNA strand, or chromosome, contains hundreds of individual genes. When living things reproduce, they share their genes with their offspring. Because dogs are directly descended from wolves, wolves and dogs share a lot of the same genes.

Sexual reproduction—The genetic lottery

In the beginning, life reproduced *asexually*—an amoeba reproduces, for example, by simply splitting in half, producing two "daughter" amoebas genetically identical to the "mother" amoeba. This method of reproduction is very simple, requires no specialized structures, and can be done in the absence of another member of the same species. Unfortunately, it has some drawbacks, the primary disadvantage being a lack of variation between individuals. If a single amoeba splits into two identical daughter cells, and each of those daughter cells splits into two identical daughter cells, and so on and so on, one will eventually have hundreds of thousands of daughter amoebas, each one identical to the original mother amoeba and to each other. Should the mother amoeba have some sort of genetic problem which causes "her" to burst unexpectedly at the age of twenty-eight hours, all her daughters will also have the same problem. Likewise, if a predator arises which enjoys feeding on the mother amoeba and things that taste like her, none of the daughters will have any options for predator avoidance that the mother amoeba did not have, because they are all alike. Genetic variation in asexually reproducing species occurs only through spontaneous mutation, which is relatively rare.

Wolves and dogs and humans, as well as a lot of other lucky species, reproduce *sexually*—they have two genders, each of which produces one type of specialized sex cell. These sex cells merge, at conception, to form a new organism. Each offspring receives two copies of every gene—one copy from the animal's mother and one from its father. This means that a mother wolf, for example, needs a father wolf to fertilize her eggs in order to reproduce—she cannot reproduce alone—and every single one of her offspring will be different from her and from the father wolf and (with the exception of identical twins) from each other. The population of wolves will be highly variable compared to a population of asexually reproducing amoeba and, should disease or a change in the environment come along, it will be much more likely that at least one member of the population of wolves will have an assortment of genes which will allow it to handle the situation.

Genetic information is carried from parent to offspring by specialized sex cells called *gametes* (eggs and sperm). In dogs and wolves, each gamete contains exactly 39 chromosomes—half of the adult complement of DNA. It will combine with the gamete from the other parent to form a fertilized egg with 78 chromosomes in 39 matched pairs—a full set of DNA, with two copies of each gene, one coming from the chromosomes contained in the egg, and one copy from those in the sperm.

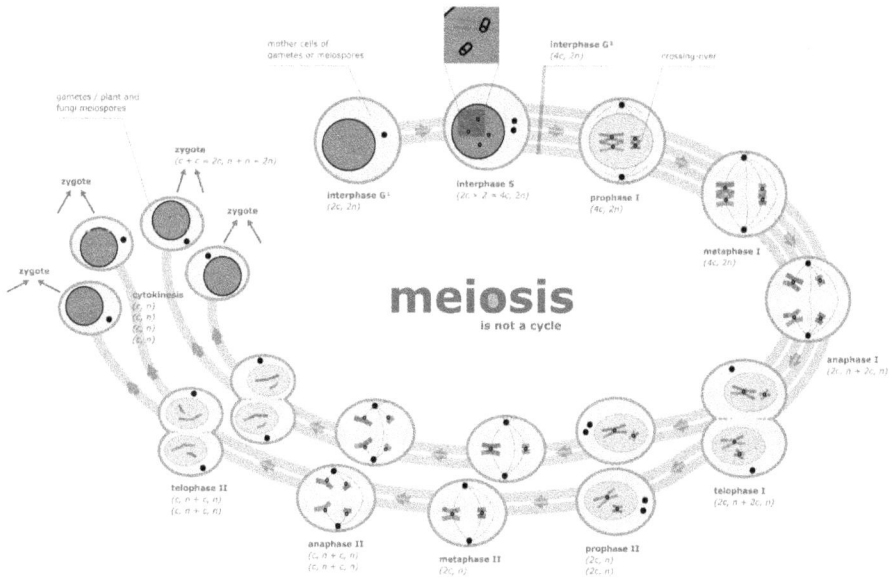

The process of meiosis, through which gametes are produced. Source: Marek Kultys, Wikimedia Commons.

The egg and sperm are formed via a process called *meiosis*, in which a cell with the full complement of 78 chromosomes makes a duplicate copy of its DNA, shuffles it around somewhat, and then splits in half twice, forming four gametes, each with a randomly assorted fifty percent of the genetic information of the original cell (see illustration above). The genetic information contained in the new gametes is randomly assorted during meiosis. The 39 pairs of chromosomes dance around, "picking" a side randomly, and occasionally even exchange their copies of individual genes. This complicated process of assortment assures that no two gametes from one individual contain exactly the same genetic information. This process happens in every sexually reproducing living thing—including humans—and is the source of a great deal of the variation in those living things.

Picture a "grab bag" full of all of the potential parental genes available, from which each gamete is allowed to pull one random copy of each gene. No two eggs from the mother and no two sperm from the father will end up grabbing exactly the same set of genes from the bag. Because of this, two puppies in the same litter will not be genetically identical, but will display an assortment of behavioral and physiological traits (Willems, 1993). (True identical twins result from the accidental division of a fertilized egg into two identical fertilized eggs, which both develop into genetically identical embryos.) Because a litter is formed from the combination of several different sperm with several different eggs, each pup in a litter will be a unique representative of aspects of both its father and its mother.

Alleles: Dominance and recessiveness

"[W]izarding ability is inherited in a Mendelian fashion, with the wizard allele (W) being recessive to the muggle allele (M)."

~ Jeffrey M. Craig, et al., in "Harry Potter and the Recessive Allele"

Every gene comes in a variety of "flavors," or versions, called *alleles*. Each individual chromosome carries only one allele, one version, of each gene. Most cells contain two copies of each chromosome, and therefore two copies, or two alleles, of each gene. One allele of each gene comes from each parent, from the *haploid* (having half the normal complement of DNA) egg and sperm. An animal may have two copies of the same allele or two different alleles, depending on the genetics of the parents.

Alleles differ in how they are expressed, or exhibited, by the animal. Some alleles are *dominant* to other alleles, which means that if the puppy has two different alleles of a single gene, the dominant one will be expressed and the *recessive* (non-dominant) allele will not be expressed. Common alleles or alleles which have unique or striking effects are often given names by the scientists who work with them. Dominant alleles are usually named with capital letters, and recessive alleles with small letters.

		Maternal	
		B	b
Paternal	B	BB	Bb
	b	Bb	bb

The possible combination of alleles from an individual's parents.

For example, the gene which codes for coat color in Labradors comes in two alleles: "B," which codes for "B"lack fur, and "b," which codes for chocolate, or "b"rown, fur. A puppy inherits one copy of the color gene from its mother, and one from its father, ending up with a genetic "code" (or *genotype*) like this: "BB" (inheriting a B allele from both mother and father), "Bb" (inheriting a B allele from one parent and a b allele from the other), or "bb" (inheriting a b allele from both parents).

B is dominant to b, which means that the effects of the B allele are expressed preferentially to those of any b alleles which may be present. A puppy with the "BB" genotype has two copies of the dominant B allele, and will be black. So will a puppy with the "Bb" genotype. Its dominant B allele overrides the effects of the b allele and the puppy's fur will also be black. A puppy with two b alleles ("bb") has no dominant B gene to make its fur black and so will express the effects of the b allele resulting in chocolate colored fur.

Dominance and recessiveness is only the tip of the iceberg in the interaction of genes and alleles. The coat color of yellow Labradors is actually produced by the effects of another, completely separate gene from the one that determines black or chocolate coat color. The dominant allele of this *epistatic gene* (a gene which alters the expression of other genes) does not directly change the "B" or "b" coat color gene. The two genes continue to exist as normal. However, if a dog receives two copies of the recessive allele of the epistatic gene (an "ee" genotype), the effect of the two "e" alleles totally overrides, or *masks*, the effects of the "B" or "b" coat color gene. This condition produces an animal with yellow fur, no matter what color the coat color gene actually codes for in that animal. Yellow Labradors still have the "B" or "b" gene for coat color, but the presence of the two copies ("ee") of the recessive allele of the epistatic gene masks the effect of the B and b alleles.

Sound complicated? That's actually part of the point. As will be explained below, what an animal actually looks like is a product of many, many different genes, and is in fact a very unreliable way to gather information about the potential ancestry of a wolf or a dog.

"Wolf" genes and "dog" genes

A high school Mendelian genetics course will tell you that the offspring of two individuals will, in general, be "midway" between its parents on all extremes: height, weight, and even behavior. It is difficult to determine what "midway" means, however, between two animals whose looks and behaviors are so similar they can actually overlap.

When a pure wolf breeds with a pure dog, the gametes from mother and father each contain a random assortment of 50% of the genetic material from that parent. In theory, this means that the offspring will inherit fifty percent "wolf" genes and 50% "dog" genes. However, this does not mean that the offspring have exactly 50% of their genes telling them to be "wolf-like" and 50% of their genes telling them to be "dog-like." Since dogs and wolves are so closely related, there is hardly such a thing as "dog" genes and "wolf" genes.

Wolves and dogs are almost identical, genetically speaking. Their DNA is still so similar that they can produce viable offspring together. Most of the changes effected to create the dog from the wolf are mere simple modifications of the "original" wolf genes. "Midway" between any one "dog" gene and its "wolf" counterpart may not be much of a change from either (Willems, 1995).

The physiology and behavior of both animals are so closely related, any differences we see might be caused by only the tiniest of changes in actual genetic code—or might be caused by environment, learning, a combination of many factors, or something else entirely. The difference between any two individual genes might be so subtle, a pure dog puppy that somehow received exactly one gene from a pure wolf might never notice any difference.

Genetics compounded and confounded: Genes affecting each other

So far, even this relatively simplified view of genetics is already becoming rather cumbersome. Further complicating this already many-faceted notion is the fact that most characteristics are actually coded for by several genes working in tandem. As we have seen with coat color in Labradors, some genes can change the effects of other genes. Mendel certainly had it easy with his peas! The most famous example of multiple genes interacting to affect a characteristic in an animal is the Belyaev "silver fox farm" experiment cited in the previous chapter. In that experiment, Belyaev attempted to breed foxes solely for the one quality of tolerance of humans (so they could be more easily handled by fur farmers). His efforts produced animals which were indeed tolerant of humans, but which were *also* spotted, floppy-eared, curly-tailed, or had underbites and overbites. These traits apparently just "popped up" as the foxes were being bred for tolerance of humans. What we know now is that breeding solely for how friendly an animal is toward humans changed the expression of other genes coded for jaw formation, fur color, tail shape, and more. Imagine how many genes must be interacting to produce the quality of "friendliness."

A silver phase red fox, like the subjects of Belyaev's famous study. Photo courtesy of Monty Sloan.

Several genes combine, for example, to create the serotonin molecule (serotonin is a calming hormone which plays a role in friendliness). These genes code for the shape of the molecule, how much of it to produce, where in the body to send it, under what environmental circumstances to produce it, and how effectively various tissues absorb it. Together, all those genes impact how much serotonin is produced and absorbed by the animal and how much it affects the animal's behavior. The "wolf" gene for serotonin shape probably looks a lot like the "dog" gene, since they both use serotonin in roughly the same way. The "wolf" gene governing serotonin production, however, may instruct the body to produce less of it than the "dog" gene does. Likewise, the "dog" gene for the timing of serotonin production may induce the body to produce serotonin more often than the "wolf" gene. Some of the genes, once combined in the fertilized egg in a wolf x dog mating, may affect genes from the other parent in unpredictable ways—altering them subtly or radically, changing the proteins they produce or the way they interact with other genes. In addition, all these genes are located in several spots on various chromosomes and nothing guarantees that a puppy will get all the serotonin-related genes from either the wolf parent or the dog parent.

A theoretical "50%" hybrid puppy, depending on the selection of genes she gets from each parent, can have "wolf" serotonin production, "dog" serotonin production, or a combination of the two which may be a midline between them or which may act in a completely unpredictable fashion. And, serotonin production is hardly the only process affecting behavior; hundreds of thousands of genes combine, each time a fertilized egg is formed, to create a completely unique puppy with a completely unique set of genes, interacting in a completely unique way.

Fractious fractions: Percentages

In this chapter, we have referred to offspring produced when a purebred wolf mates with a purebred dog as "50%" hybrids—animals with 50% dog genes and 50% wolf genes. Elsewhere in this text, we refer to animals which were "25% wolf" or "100% wolf." What does this notation mean, and where does it come from?

People commonly use percentages to try to denote how much wolf ancestry is in a particular animal. A wolf, of course, is considered to have 100% wolf ancestry. A dog has no recent wolf ancestry. Simply add the amount of wolf ancestry in the parents and divide by two. Therefore, a wolf (100%) mated to a dog (0%) produces 50% puppies. Mate one of those 50% puppies to a pure wolf (100%) and you will get 75% wolf puppies. This is called the "pedigree method" of calculating wolf percentage.

However, the previously discussed aspects of wolf and dog genetics make it prohibitively difficult to accurately predict the adult looks and behavior of any individual wolf hybrid puppy, even when parental heritage is known and percentages are calculated. Even in the simplest of crossings (100% wolf x 100% dog, producing 50% hybrid puppies), exactly *which* 50% each puppy gets from which parent will vary from puppy to puppy. In terms of behavior, a 50% wolf heritage does not mean that the animal will act like a wolf or like a dog only half the time. All one can do is to make an educated guess that these hypothetical 50% puppies will act "something like a wolf, and something like a dog, and something in between," but that is an awfully vague concept to be applied to animals one hopes to have living in one's home, interacting with one's spouse and/or children.

The variation increases exponentially the further one gets from that first wolf/dog mating. For example, an animal born to a 50% wolf and a "pure" dog is technically 25% wolf. However, again, that does not put any firm quota on how much it will look or act like a wolf, nor does it guarantee that the animal will look or act like a dog 75% of the time. There is no way to govern, predict, or measure exactly which genes will come from which parent, and what effect they will have when combined with the genes from the other parent. Beyond that, not every breeder uses the "pedigree method" to assign percentages to his or her animals. Some assign percentages based solely on the looks or behavior of the animal, regardless of their genetics. Some assign whatever percentage makes the animal legal to own or sell in that location (a "99% wolf hybrid" may be legal in places where a "100% wolf" is not), and some assign whatever fetches the highest price.

This makes percentages inaccurate, and sometimes even misleading, when it comes to describing, predicting, or legislating about wolf hybrids. When the phrase "50% wolf" can describe an animal which looks and acts just like a wolf, an animal which looks and acts just like a dog, or anything in between, how can one expect to use percentages—or genetics at all—to predict how best to train or manage the animal, not to mention enact any meaningful legislation to protect the public?

Chapter 5

Variable Outcomes: It's Not That Simple

We have now explored in a fair amount of detail what makes a wolf a wolf and what makes a dog a dog. We know that an animal's genes, inherited from its parents, play a significant role in determining what the animal looks like and how it behaves. We have seen how the forces of evolution (remember the peppered moth?) can impact animals over time and how domestication and selective breeding can bring about change much more quickly than evolution working alone. Alas, despite having demonstrated several ways in which the relationship between wolves and dogs is complicated at the genetic level, we are not yet done. There are a number of other variables at work as well, and some of them may surprise you—including nutrition, age, line breeding, and something we call the "zebra effect."

Confounding variables

In this highly confusing and complex world, we rely on our perception of patterns, both real and imagined, previously encountered in familiar objects in order to make guesses about the nature of unknown things. At some point in our lives, armed with images from the media, anecdotes from friends, and possibly some experiences of our own, we create a mental "pattern" of traits which tell us, when detected, that *this animal is a wolf*. These physical characteristics, when manifested in an animal, fire off our "this is a wolf" recognition system, and—aha! —we find that we are seeing a wolf.

This "guessing" system can be very useful in the wild, as we generalize from having seen one snake to being able to recognize anything long, cylindrical, and thin as possibly being another snake, instead of having to thoroughly investigate every new object from scratch, to examine its properties and see if it bites. However, as anyone who has mistaken a broken fan belt on the side of the road for a wandering anaconda knows, our "guessing" system can sometimes leap to the wrong conclusion, and fire off a SNAKE! warning signal when all we are looking at is a worn section of garden hose. "Long, cylindrical, and thin" can describe a lot of things, not just snakes. "Yellow eyes and big feet" can describe a wolf—or a lion, or an owl. Variation between individuals makes it very hard to generalize that *every* snake looks like *this*, or that *every* wolf looks like *that*. Our "guessing" system is a highly useful tool for finding answers to immediate, urgent questions like, *"What have I just stepped on?"* Unfortunately, however, it is not always accurate. Immediate impressions of physical appearance do not always allow us to draw correct conclusions about an animal's ancestry.

Individual variation in physical shape

As researchers (and human parents of twins) have known for years, even animals which are completely genetically identical and raised in the same environment will not turn out to be precisely identical behaviorally. The action of environmental factors can never be precisely identical between two individuals and must, necessarily, occupy slightly different positions in space and time. The result of this slightly different environment can lead to variations in behavior between genetically identical individuals. Even in populations of essentially genetically identical individuals such as highly inbred laboratory rats and mice, some of the animals are bolder, shyer, more or less active, more or less aggressive, etc.

Note the variation between these two black phase wolves. The one in front has "silvered" with age. Photo courtesy of Monty Sloan.

The variation in individuals who are *not* genetically identical can be huge. Wolves, as mentioned earlier, tend to live under very similar environmental pressures (must hunt to eat, must fight to reproduce, etc.). They therefore tend to have very generally similar genetics, appearance, and behavior, even between different subspecies. Even within a litter of pure wolf puppies, however, there can be considerable variation, both physical and behavioral (Zimen, 1987; Fox, 1972). Some pups will grow to be taller, others wider, some will have more black in their fur (or be completely black), some will have eyes that turn gold, yellow, or even orange, while some will have eyes which stay almost green. Some will have tails that curl a little more or a little less, some will jump higher, run faster, have a particularly low, musical howl, or perhaps have lips that turn up at the corners just a very little, giving them a permanent "smile."

In dogs, this physiological plasticity is extraordinarily pronounced. The extreme morphological variability of the dog has for hundreds of years been confounding those who have been working with purebred dogs, trying to produce animals which conform to "breed standards" or descriptions of an ideal member of that breed. This means that, despite the best efforts of breeders, purebred Labrador Retrievers are not all the spitting image of their breed ideal. As Patricia B. McConnell says in her excellent book *The Other End of the Leash,* not all purebred dogs seem to have read the appropriate AKC breed description. For example, a significant percentage of Labrador Retrievers carry two copies of the recessive allele of an important gene or two (remember the epistatic "ee" gene?). This results in dogs with yellow coats and pink noses and lips, a very lovely color combination aesthetically, but one that cannot even be registered with the AKC because it is not in the breed standard. They are still considered to be Labrador Retrievers, however.

A yellow coated Labrador Retriever. Photo by Jessica Addams.

Different bloodlines of each breed have been created as human uses for the breed, or even just fashion, have changed. German Shepherds come in a huge variety of shapes and colors, depending on the use one may plan for the animal. For example, "show" bloodlines stick close to the AKC breed description, while "guard" dogs may be more compact and muscular or, depending on preference, much, much larger. "Pet" varieties may almost resemble the Labrador Retriever in size, shape, and personality. The Shepherd breed standard has also changed over time, and Shepherds may have more or less of their distinctive low hip carriage, tails of differing length or shape, a white coat, longer fur, etc., depending on what bloodline they are from and which breed standard their individual breeder liked most.

A white German Shepherd. Photo courtesy of Monty Sloan.

A traditionally colored German Shepherd. Photo courtesy of Monty Sloan.

A long-haired German Shepherd. Photo courtesy of Karoliina Toivanen, through Flickr Creative Commons.

A purebred German Shepherd with a single floppy ear, an example of individual variation. Photo courtesy of Monty Sloan.

An educational look at variation within a breed is presented at www.huskycolors.com, a web site showcasing owner photographs of many Huskies. These purebred dogs display coat colors from white to black with every variation in between, including spotted, brindle, and wolf-like agouti. Physically, they have blue eyes and brown eyes and gold eyes. They are tall, short, thin, fat, straight-tailed and curly-tailed, with long coats and short coats. All this variation appears in only one breed! Imagine a long-coated black-and-white spotted Husky breeding with a short-coated agouti Husky. Imagine what the offspring of two wolf-like agouti animals might look like or be mistaken for!

Spontaneous mutations

Sometimes the complicated machinery which copies DNA molecules breaks down, and an egg or sperm is created with a "coding problem" at one or more genes. Often, the mis-translation does not affect gene expression, and the resulting offspring looks completely normal. Occasionally, however, the miscoding messes with a gene which codes for some big, visible, obvious trait, and produces an offspring which exhibits some unusual qualities. Any species may produce a "sport," an unusual, but otherwise purebred dog (or wolf, gorilla, or cockatoo) with a spontaneous mutation which sets it apart from other animals in its class. Albinism, unexpectedly floppy or pointy ears, blue or green or yellow eyes, a strangely curled (or straight) tail or no tail at all, spots, brindling, and other unusual color patterns are all examples of possible results of spontaneous mutation.

Spontaneous mutation is relatively rare, but it happens often enough. For example, many of the carefully line-bred mice used in research today are descendants of one animal which had a spontaneous mutation in some vital gene. The "Pound Mouse," bred (and copyrighted) by Charles River Laboratories, is a breed of mouse descended from a small group of closely related mice, who all had copies of a gene with a spontaneous mutation. All descended from a single ancestor, the mice had a mutation in the gene which codes for receptors in cells which bond with leptin, a hormone which regulates energy intake and output. The lack of functioning leptin receptors causes Pound Mice to become obese while being fed the same diet as mice who have functioning leptin receptors. Researchers use the Pound Mouse as a model for the study of human obesity. Several different research mouse lineages are based on such spontaneous mutations.

Unusual dogs, or "sports," who have one or more strange mutations, or who are simply not the shape or color preferred by the breeder—do not simply vanish when they appear. They may be culled by the breeder, but they are also often taken into homes and kept as pets. Sometimes someone takes a fancy to the unique attribute and deliberately breeds the dog, creating a "rare bloodline" of those animals which may sell for considerably more than the standard version (consider the white Doberman, or the "Merle" Border Collie).

A Merle Border Collie. Photo courtesy of Monty Sloan.

These animals are still considered to be members of their original breed, even though they look completely different (white fur, blue eyes, etc.). Thus, it is possible to find, say, a Siberian Husky which looks almost exactly like a wolf, because of some "sport" mutation which caused it to have unusually small or furry ears, or an uncurled tail, or an agouti coat. It would still be a Husky, but it would look like something else, because of that one random mutation somewhere in its genetic past.

A northern breed dog with very wolflike coloration. Photo courtesy of Ryan Talbot.

Because of the strong selection pressures imposed on them, wild wolves have a relatively low incidence of "sports" which survive to adulthood. In captivity, of course, the percentage would be higher, but wolves do not produce "sports" as often as the amazingly genetically plastic dog.

Inbreeding and line breeding

"Family trees should branch." ~ Dr. Julia Becker, DVM

"Sports" occur through other avenues as well. In order to obtain more animals with a desired genetic property, such as a white coat, blue eyes, or a tendency to herd sheep, breeders have been practicing "line breeding" (a modified form of inbreeding) for hundreds of years. Breeding related animals together tends to pull not normally expressed recessive or unusual genes to the surface and allows them to be displayed. In this way, one can make sure that a beneficial mutation (at least in the eye of the breeder), such as a peculiarly beautiful color pattern or an exceptional ability to track, race, or hunt, will be passed on to as many offspring as possible. Once a breeding line of animals consistently exhibits a trait, it is said to be "fixed" in that population and will breed true.

While inbreeding and line breeding bring recessive traits to the surface and "fix" them in a population, not all the recessive traits which appear are necessarily good ones. Just as breeding for "tolerance of humans" brings out unrelated characteristics like floppy ears or curled tails, breeding for other traits like a white coat or blue eyes can bring out traits for which one did not intend to breed. The patterns of line breeding in German Shepherds, for example, gave them their distinctive physical look, as well as an unfortunate tendency toward hip dysplasia, a disorder with genetic causes. Highly inbred lines (of both animals and humans) tend to produce stock with unfortunate physical defects, such as shortened muzzles (or chins), overbites and underbites, and disorders such as hereditary deafness or hemophilia (Laikre and Ryman, 1991; Laikre et al., 1993).

Line breeding and inbreeding can be strong factors in the creation of purebred animals, but they can occur in wild populations as well. Wolves in the wild do not often breed with their kin (although, in captivity, they may have no choice), but it does sometimes occur, and so wild populations can produce offspring with some of these unfortunate hereditary malformations. In wolves, inbreeding can cause deformations such as shortened muzzles, domed foreheads, brachycephalic heads, "fubsy" or infantile plump bodies with short legs, or "corkscrew" tails. In this way, one can encounter pure wolves which appear, at first glance, to be shaped like some of the more unique breeds of dog—or, at least, not like wolves are commonly expected to look. We once visited the Halliburton Forest Wolf Centre in Canada, which had at the time a very inbred pack, all descended from two individuals, Trats and Wen. The pack had several adult members with shortened muzzles and slightly domed foreheads. They were pure wolves, but looked very different from the wolf "standard."

The wolves on Isle Royale, which is a small, isolated ecosystem, are also inbred, and are showing increasing evidence of congenitally malformed vertebrae caused by inbreeding (Räikkönen et al., 2009). Likewise, the small (only one hundred individuals) Scandinavian wolf population, descended from only three founding animals in 1983, suffers similar problems (Räikkönen et al., 2006). All these animals are generally considered to be pure wolves, but you might not know it just from looking at their skeletons. For many years, as well, Wolf Park had on display an inbred female wolf with a severely shortened muzzle and unusually domed head. She was pure wolf—and acted like it—but did not look at all like a typical wolf.

Aurora, a pure wolf at Wolf Park, with a highly unusual head shape due to inbreeding. Photo courtesy of Monty Sloan.

Nutrition, aging, injury, and disease impacting appearance

Dogs and wolves (like most animals) change shape drastically between birth and adulthood. They move from the "furry slug" stage at puppyhood—with huge head and belly and tiny, short legs—to adulthood, with (usually) longer legs, a relatively smaller head, and of course a much larger size overall. The muzzle and ears grow proportionally larger, the eyes develop, the legs get larger and longer, and the paws and tail get proportionally bigger.

A pure wolf pup whose ears have not yet "risen," giving her a dog-like appearance. Photo courtesy of Monty Sloan.

This process of growth and change can be altered by outside influences as well as by the original genetics of the animal. A notable non-genetic influence is nutrition, which under ordinary circumstances provides the developing young animal with the energy and materials it needs to change its shape and create new body mass. Lack of sufficient, balanced nutrition—especially in calcium, phosphorus, and vitamin D—during the critical growth phase can produce unusually small, "stunted" individuals, unusually tall individuals or malformed bone growth (as in rickets). This can result in an animal whose physiology differs markedly from the expected breed standard.

5 — VARIABLE OUTCOMES: IT'S NOT THAT SIMPLE

A juvenile black-phase gray wolf with dark markings, and the especially plush first-winter coat of a yearling wolf. Photo courtesy of Monty Sloan.

An elderly black-phase wolf, faded to silvery white, with puffy face and curly outer coat, products of aging. Photo courtesy of Monty Sloan.

Aging also affects an animal's looks. Wolves generally get lighter as they age, with gray animals becoming almost or entirely white and black animals acquiring first white patches of increasing size and later an overall gray or silver shade which can resemble the single-tone coats of dogs. Eye color can darken with age, especially in environments with relatively little shade. Age and disease can both affect how animals shed, making fur look more rough or giving it unusual patterns. Age reduces muscle tone, sometimes making an animal appear to be a different shape than it was in its prime. The skin on the head will sag and droop, changing the apparent shape of the muzzle and head. Very old animals can look nothing like they did when they were young.

Injuries can change the shape of an animal in ways both large and small. Flies often cluster on the ears of canids during the summer months. The action of these flies can be so severe that pointed ears are rendered rounded, or the ear tips removed altogether.

An older animal with damaged, shortened ears. Photo courtesy of Ryan Talbot.

Frostbite or fighting injuries can change the shape of ears or lips or feet. An injury to a limb can warp the body of the animal as it compensates for the lack of support from that leg, or simply change the animal's gait to make it look unusual in some way. An old, healed break in the tail can alter its shape or carriage. Even the negligible "injury" of sunburn can change the color of an animal's facial skin. Sun can also alter the color of its fur (such as the fur of black animals "burning" orange in the summer with sun exposure).

Ultimately there are a number of different factors that can affect the physiology of an animal, whether it be physical injury, disease, malnutrition, aging, or some combination of the above. All of these further contribute to the unpredictability of the adult behaviors and phenotype of an animal.

Dog breeds bred to resemble wolves

Since the gamut of dog variation overlaps that of the wolf (Coppinger and Coppinger, 1998), it is inevitable that some dogs will look and act like wolves to varying degrees. Some breeds have even been specifically selected for traits which, at least superficially, resemble those of wolves.

A Siberian Husky puppy. Photo courtesy of Monty Sloan.

Siberian Huskies and Malamutes in particular seem to be popularly considered to resemble wolves and are also, not coincidentally, the most popular dog breeds to cross with wolves to make hybrids. Huskies and Malamutes are not the spitting images of wolves—they have smaller feet, wider chests, smaller heads, and characteristic "mask" markings which are different than those of wolves—but they resemble wolves closely enough to give a layperson pause to consider. Both breeds have short, pointed ears, a thick, double fur coat that "blows out" (sheds) in the summer, a tendency toward agouti ("wolfy") fur patterns, and behavior which tends to the more independent side. To someone who has not worked personally with many wolves, Huskies and Malamutes often resemble wolves.

Inuit dogs. Photo courtesy of Monty Sloan.

The Inuit dog, and variations thereof, is being bred to resemble the hardy, intelligent animals that Native Americans used for hunting, transportation, and companionship. These bright, beautiful animals often have a lot of Husky and Malamute blood in them (as well as, arguably, some wolf way back in their pedigrees), and many have striking and unusual markings. A lot of them retain the independent behavior of their Husky and Malamute lineage. Since they resemble no common dog breed—and, indeed, often do not even closely resemble each other—many people assume these animals are wolves or wolf hybrids (or dog/coyote hybrids) simply because they are so unusual that they "cannot possibly" be a purebred dog.

Overseas, a number of different people have worked on trying to make "dogs that look like wolves"—pure dogs with very dog-like behavior, but wolf-like looks. The "Czechoslovakian Wolf-Dog" (Ceskoslovensky Vlcak) is a dog breed registered with the American Kennel Club. The animals strongly resemble wolves physically (because they have been deliberately bred to do so) but, behaviorally, they are all dog.

A Czechoslovakian Wolf-Dog, a pure dog bred to physically resemble a wolf. Photo courtesy of Monty Sloan.

Although it is true that some of these dog breeds do have wolves in their relatively recent ancestry, wolves are generally no longer being actively used in the breeding program. The current breeding stock consists of animals that are many generations removed from any original wolves and hybrids and by now, the animals are genetically one hundred percent dog. Remember, *all* dogs have wolf in their ancestry; it's just a matter of how far back on the pedigree it is. (As Ray Coppinger says, "All people have Charlemagne in their ancestry—so what?")

Other breeds which can produce individuals that can be readily mistaken for wolves include the Laika, the Sarloos Wolfhound (which also has some relatively recent wolf ancestry, but is essentially 100% dog), the Norwegian Elkhound, the Canadian Eskimo Dog, the Greenland Dog, and the Samoyed. Members of the German Shepherd breed are also often mistaken for wolves, because of the Shepherd's impressive size, its sometimes agouti-like coloration, and its occasionally aggressive or territorial behavior, which can seem unusually intense to someone more familiar with the behavior of, say, the Cocker Spaniel. White German Shepherds, because they are not always commonly known, are often misidentified as Arctic wolves or Arctic wolf hybrids.

The mutt factor

"A mutt is couture—it's the only one like it in the world, made especially for you."
~ Julia Szabo, pet columnist

So far our focus has been on "pure" breeds, highly identifiable bloodlines of dog with reasonably reliable similarities between individual members of the breed. They are certainly not the only representatives of the dog, however. Since dogs do not generally require the help of humans to reproduce, there are also a considerable number of "mutts" running about adding their own contribution to the genetic puzzle. Any two physically compatible dogs can mate and produce offspring. And so can their offspring, producing "breeds" like the "Labradoodle" and "Cockapoo," and then mixes of those animals and mixes of *those* animals, coming out with an eventual proud member of the "Heinz 57" breed, in which the genetic history of the animal is anyone's guess. These animals occasionally resemble the ancestral wolf (as well as the not-so-ancestral "dust mop").

Contrary to general opinion, it is not always easy to pick out the two (or more) breeds which make up a mutt, even when the breeds were relatively dissimilar (a Labrador Retriever and a Poodle, for example, or a wolf and a German Shepherd). The "close relatedness" factor making the wolf and dog genomes nearly identical is exponentially increased when one combines two breeds of dog, and the nearly infinite possibilities for genetic interaction (and spontaneous mutation) mean that one may be looking for a long time for a definitive answer about whether one's puppy received its enormous ears from mom, dad, spontaneous mutation, or a distant ancestor whose genetic contribution has only just surfaced. (There are DNA tests available which claim to solve just this very problem. Their effectiveness will be discussed later in this book.)

Litters sired by different fathers

Reproduction is not always as simple as one egg meeting with one sperm. A female canid does not necessarily have all of her eggs available for fertilization at the exact same time. The "ripe" eggs are released into the uterus over time. Estrous behavior and mating may begin long before ovulation (Phemister et al., 1973) and sperm, which in canines is remarkably sturdy, can "hang around" in the uterus "waiting" for eggs to be later released if mating occurs before ovulation (Evans, 1933). These circumstances can result in litters with more than one sire, as eggs released at different times are fertilized by sperm from more than one mating which is "waiting" in the uterus for the arrival of the eggs.

Multiple paternity is a common enough occurrence that the AKC has registration forms especially for litters with multiple sires. If one (or more) of the matings happened accidentally (fences don't mean quite as much to canids when somebody in estrous is on the other side), it is possible one could have a litter with mixed parentage and not even know it.

For evidence of multiple paternity in various wild canids, see: Glenn et al., 2009, Randall et al., 2007; Carmichael et al., 2007; Baker et al., 2004; and Sillero-Zubiri et al., 1996.

That is not my little doggie

> *"The identity of one changes with how one perceives reality."*
> ~ Vithu Jeyaloganathan, author

A further confounding factor is the occasional misinformation circulating about various dog breeds. Misunderstandings arise between seller and purchaser. Dogs are given away with incomplete or inaccurate information. Mutts of all kinds are adopted from shelters, not always with pedigree intact, and we find that not every dog owner has entirely accurate information as to which breed their animal really is. Janis Bradley, in *Dogs Bite, but Balloons and Slippers are More Dangerous*, writes of a lady in one of her puppy classes who was convinced that her Samoyed puppy was a Shitz Tzu. Particularly rare breeds may also be misidentified as crosses. Patricia McConnell writes about a family in *The Other End of the Leash* whose "Dachshund/terrier cross" turned out to be a picture-perfect Petit Basset Griffon Vendéen.

A Petit Basset Griffon Vendéen. Photo courtesy of mljones1, through Flickr Creative Commons.

Shelters commonly find that the vast majority of their clients have knowledge of just a few popular dog breeds. These include (but are not limited to) the Labrador, the "terrier" (not actually a breed, but a type), the German Shepherd, and the "pit bull" (an unfortunate "breed" in its own right and victim of the same kind of flurry of misinformation and misidentification as the wolf hybrid). These familiar breeds cover a wide range of possible physical characteristics and, therefore, are often (mis)identified as parental contributors in mixed-breed dogs. Any smaller animal with a short muzzle and wiry hair coat becomes a "terrier" mix. Anything with floppy ears and a straight, powerful tail is a "Lab" mix. Large ears and black-and-tan coloration are the hallmarks of a "Shepherd" mix. Anything which even remotely resembles an American Staffordshire Terrier, a Bull Terrier ("Spuds MacKenzie"), or any similar breed is automatically a "pit bull" or "pit bull mix." These animals may, or may not, actually have heritage from the breeds in question, but having been labeled as such, their behavior can affect public perception of that breed whether they are a genuine member of it or not.

Likewise, the vast quantity of misinformation surrounding wolves has led a number of people to believe that their pet dog, for some reason, is a wolf or wolf hybrid. Sometimes the animal really is a wolf or hybrid, sometimes it is an oddly-colored Husky or Malamute (two more familiar breeds often misidentified) exhibiting breed-typical, independent behavior. Or, sometimes, it is just a mutt with some behavior problems. Since there is so much misinformation available about wolves, it is very difficult for the layman to produce a snap decision on an animal's true ancestry. Some animals go through their whole lives breeding and producing offspring that are erroneously labeled as "wolf" or "wolf hybrid" (or "dog"), producing litters of puppies with the same wrong label. Some experts feel that as many as one-half of all animals identified as "wolf hybrids" are actually pure dogs which only look somewhat like wolves (Siino, 1990).

The presence of these animals confounds efforts to determine the ancestry of a dog just by evaluation of physical characteristics. Consider how the offspring of a white Doberman and a pink-nosed yellow Labrador might look. Consider the result of a breeding between a "Heinz 57" dog (a West Highland White Terrier misidentified as a Maltese) to an inbred German Shepherd with a severely shortened muzzle, or a wolf, or a wolf hybrid. What might the resultant offspring resemble?

If physical attributes are so difficult to predict and exhibit so much variation, imagine trying to predict behavioral attributes!

"Dog" behavior overlaps "wolf" behavior

A young wolf comes with a set of "installed" behaviors which allow an adult animal to interact properly with a survival-oriented world in which it must hunt live prey. A dog puppy comes with *the same set of behaviors* installed, however domestication has often altered that set of behaviors so that they may not manifest fully. Some behaviors may manifest in some cases *more* fully or may manifest in a different pattern. How the behaviors are expressed and what makes the dog demonstrate them may be the same as or different than in wolves.

For example, both young wolves and young dogs come "hard-wired" with the basic pattern for catching prey, but in wolves it is generally much more developed, because they have the "original" set of genes from the wild animal. In dogs, the pattern may "derail" halfway through, "stick" on a certain step, or even have one or more steps grossly exaggerated (the source of "pointing" in some breeds, or herding behavior in Border Collies).

Innate patterns of behavior may not only be altered by domestication, but may be "mixed" with other behaviors in unusual ways. One of us personally knows a dog whose greeting behavior has been curiously mixed with hunting behavior. When presented with humans, the dog will crouch, stalk them, rush them—classic predatory behavior—and then bound up, grinning and tail wagging, for petting in a classical friendly greeting.

Dogs are fairly likely to exhibit behaviors also exhibited by wolves. Generally, the primary difference in expression of behaviors by wolves and dogs is in *degree* of expression. How emphatic is the behavior? How often is it expressed? To whom is it expressed? Both wolves and dogs make a "bark" noise, but the expression of barking behavior differs strongly in degree. Wolves rarely bark because it is an expression of deep agitation or fear and they pull it out only for special occasions of real concern. Dogs bark all the time, and the bark is an expression of general arousal—it can indicate fear, excitement, boredom, or territory defense. However, since both wolves and dogs do bark, barking can hardly be classified as just a "wolf" behavior or a "dog" behavior. What one *can* say is that a higher *degree* of expression of barking behavior—barking more often, and at more varied targets or times—is strongly indicative of dog ancestry.

Similarly, both wolves and dogs howl, although many people do not associate howling with dogs because the environments in which most dogs find themselves do not lend themselves to the a display of "wolf-typical" howling behavior. Dogs raised singly or in urban environments where they do not regularly interact with lots of other dogs often do not display the same frequency of howling behavior (or other behaviors) as dogs (such as groups of sled dogs) raised in more "natural" social environments with many members of the same species (*conspecifics*), with which to interact (Coppinger, personal communication). Most people have experience primarily with urban dogs and their relatively subdued howling behavior, but socially raised dogs in a group-type environment howl just as much as wolves, and for much the same reasons. Howling is both a "dog" behavior and a "wolf" behavior.

Other behaviors exhibited by both wolves and dogs include digging, hunting, escaping, guarding of territory, mates, and food, and dominance behaviors like raising hackles or staring. These behaviors are common in an adult wolf, but are not generally expected of dogs by laypeople. Dogs often display them, whether humans expect them to or not.

Age and its effects on behavior

"The soul is born old, but grows young. That is the comedy of life. And the body is born young and grows old. That is life's tragedy." ~ Oscar Wilde

Young animals are generally smaller and weaker than their parents and rely on their parents (and other pack members, if any) for protection and care. It is not in the best interest of a young animal to challenge its parents or pack mates for dominance or to exhibit aggressive behavior towards them. In general, young animals display primarily submissive behaviors towards older animals, with the percentage of confident, challenging, or dominant behaviors increasing as the animal gets older, hits puberty, and becomes a sexually mature adult.

Social interaction is also at a peak with young animals who are more curious than their older relatives and more interested in interaction, both with conspecifics and with humans. Young animals devote a much greater percentage of their time to "play" or mock behaviors than do adults and their shorter attention span and developing brain makes their behavior patterns easier to modify or "derail." This is a boon for early training—a young animal displays more varied behaviors and learns faster which behaviors are more appropriate than does an adult. (For a more in-depth exploration of the development of social behavior, read *Genetics and the Social Behavior of the Dog*, by Scott and Fuller.)

An example of individual variation, an exception to all these rules: an older animal, pure wolf, taking the time to play enthusiastically with signs on his enclosure. Photo courtesy of Monty Sloan.

A young wolf may be mistaken for a young dog through its juvenile behaviors, such as its willingness to interact with new people as well as to play with and submit to them. But as the wolf grows older, he will mature out of his puppy behaviors and become much less interested in social interaction and play and less likely to submit. A dog, which, as discussed earlier, is essentially a neotenous wolf, stays a "baby" even after he is physically all grown up, and will often exhibit cuddly, playful puppy behaviors even into adulthood.

On the other end of the scale, older animals, as their energy levels wane, often become more mellow and relaxed, and often more social towards humans as they become less able to interact with their conspecifics. Dogs are also susceptible to Alzheimer's-like symptoms as the cognitive pathways in their brain deteriorate with age (Kahn, 2008). Again, at this time, wolves may be mistaken for dogs as their behavior becomes more submissive, patient, and dog-like.

An older wolf, hard to handle in his youth, now much more mellow and friendly. Photo courtesy of Monty Sloan.

Health and nutritional impacts on behavior

Disease can affect behavior in many ways. An animal that is not feeling well is likely to reduce its activity and/or aggression level as its body uses energy to fight the disease. Animals with rickets, a degenerative bone disease caused by an imbalance of phosphorus or vitamin D, may become unusually lethargic and "mellow" due to an unwillingness to exert an aching body. Animals in pain may also become more "grumpy" or irritable and more likely to show aggression. An animal in pain may be more likely to feel threatened if cornered, and may even attack in self-defense, even attacking trusted persons.

More complicated are diseases which directly cause behavior problems, such as hormone imbalances, cerebral events such as stroke, and diseases of the brain. Hormone imbalance can do a lot of exciting things to an animal's behavior, as anyone who has worked with a female horse in estrous can attest. Neurological disease can enhance aggression, turning a formerly mellow dog indiscriminately vicious (rabies is the obvious example here), or can reduce aggression, making an intractable animal docile (also, ironically, a symptom of rabies).

Some drugs, such as phenobarbital which is commonly used to treat epilepsy, may make an animal appear overly calm, lethargic, disinterested or disoriented, and may mask an unruly temperament or problem behaviors. Dogs that have recently been on medications that are meant to treat behavioral problems may not exhibit these symptoms until after placement, as the drugs in the animal's system may mask symptoms at the time of assessment.

Dogs that are on antihistamines, steroids, sedatives—a veritable host of pharmaceutical substances—may have mildly or severely altered behavior as a direct result of the drugs that may be in their system. This does not mean that one should doubt behavior that they happen to observe in an animal, but that incidental pharmaceutical effects should always be held as a possibility in the mind of someone doing an assessment.

Improper diet can cause a variety of problematic and interruptive systems. Some diets can promote atypical behaviors in an animal, especially if the diet contains certain toxic elements (remember, food items as simple as onions are toxic to dogs and can cause severe anemia (Hu et al., 2002), so this is a more likely occurrence than one might think). Information about what the animal has been eating can only strengthen the assessor's abilities to make a fair and accurate judgment about the animal in question.

As a brief side note, there is one notable instance where diet does *not* affect behavior. An all-meat diet does not cause wolves (or dogs, cats, bears, etc.) to become vicious. The scent of blood has no frenzy effect on these animals as it does, memorably, with (some) sharks. Allowing a dog, wolf, or hybrid to eat raw meat, either as a one time treat or as a primary diet staple, does not affect its behavior in any way (other than, arguably, an increase in tail-wagging). This misconception may have come about because giving a wolf (or a dog) a high-value treat, such as a piece of raw meat or a bloody bone, may increase its propensity to food guard. Thus, handing a dog a piece of raw meat may increase the likelihood of its later exhibiting aggressive behavior to defend the high value food it now possesses. However, giving a dog or a wolf raw meat will not increase the animal's overall patterns of aggression.

Socialization

The process of conditioning an animal to interact appropriately with its environment is called socialization. Wolf mothers socialize their puppies to other wolves and to life in the pack, while human owners socialize their dog puppies to humans, to other dogs, and to life in a human home, office, or city. Socialization is a key process of making an animal, of any species, well suited for living in the environment in which it has been raised. For example, an animal socialized to living in a wolf pack with other wolves will not know how to interact properly in a human home if suddenly relocated. It will need to be re-socialized to its new environment. Similarly, if a city-raised human is abruptly dropped into the jungle, he or she will not be properly socialized to the jungle environment and may not be able to respond appropriately to its challenges.

Improper socialization (for example, being raised in an impoverished environment, without ever seeing or interacting with humans) can cause multiple behavior problems in dogs including several which can be mistaken for "wolf-like" behavior such as territoriality, fear or dominance aggression, separation anxiety, or shyness (Pierantoni and Verga, 2007). Pure dog pups, improperly socialized, can grow to exhibit these behaviors, and can be mistaken for wolves by people who have never seen a dog with these behavior problems before. Such unusual behavior, they reason, could only arise from wolf ancestry and not from abuse, lack of proper human or canine interaction at a young age, or stress.

Social factors

Interaction with other animals can change the rate or degree of expression of behavior, through social reinforcement, rank order, stress reduction or production, or other means.

Other animals can act as an inhibiting factor in displays of aggression or territorial defense. A low ranking animal is unlikely to express a high degree of dominance behaviors, at least around higher ranking animals. A young animal kept with several older, dominant animals is unlikely to guard territory, for example, because guarding territory is the prerogative of higher-ranking animals who have the right to "own" territory they can guard. Should the situation change for some reason (dominant animals dying or moving away, young animal successfully challenging for rank), the young animal, suddenly high-ranking, may then exhibit an entirely new range of behaviors, including territory guarding, scent marking, etc., in which it never dared to engage when inhibited by the presence of higher-ranking animals.

The presence of other animals can reduce or exacerbate aggressive behavior, either by calming or redirecting a single nervous individual or by a group "packing up" and achieving "critical mass" as all group members grow excited at once, fueled by each other's arousal. A single calm, dominant animal can keep several obnoxious lower-ranking animals in line, or a usually meek, quiet animal can be excited into attack by the presence of a number of aggressively aroused pack mates.

Likewise, the behavior of the animal's owner or handler can affect how the animal responds to the world (Schwab and Huber, 2006; Call et al., 2003). A shy animal with a confident handler may pick up on the human's confidence and act more boldly. An aggressive animal with a shy handler may feel that he has to take control of unusual situations, because his human will not, and will act more aggressive. A frightened animal with a frightened handler may attack in self defense if he feels his handler will not defend him. Put these animals in the hands of another handler with a different attitude, and their behavior may change radically.

Location

Animals who are in a safe, familiar location will behave differently when moved to an unfamiliar location (Klausz et al., 2009). An animal who feels it is on "home ground" is more likely to relax, rest, eat, or play, or interact confidently with new people. However, it is also more likely to feel confident enough to guard that "home ground," so it may also be more likely to exhibit territorial aggression in its home space.

An animal in an unfamiliar location is more likely to be fearful, shy, or submissive. It may even become fearfully aggressive if it is frightened enough. It may not want to rest, eat, play. New territory elicits exploratory behavior (digging, scent marking) as well. Picture your pet dog at the veterinarian's office and how her behavior there might differ from her behavior at home.

A wolf may be mistaken for a dog when it has been moved to an unfamiliar environment. It may not feel confident enough to challenge for dominance, defend its territory, or guard its possessions. It may submit to new people or be more tolerant of them—in other words, act like a dog. After time in its new residence, however, its confidence may grow and it may become more likely to exhibit those behaviors that are more typical of a wolf. In the same sort of way, a dog may be mistaken for a wolf when in an unfamiliar environment—it may feel threatened and feel that it needs to assert itself over humans or other dogs, displaying more dominant behaviors than it usually would. Otherwise, it might feel frightened in a new place, and display a great deal of avoidance and fear behavior, leading people to believe it was behaving like a wild animal.

The zebra effect

"For every complex problem, there is a solution that is simple, neat, and wrong."
~ H. L. Mencken

A last, and not often considered confounding factor in the misidentification of canids, which has little to do with the environment and more to do with the psychology of the observer, is the zebra effect. In school, young doctors and nurses, eager to be the first to diagnose some mysterious new ailment in their patients, must be counseled to look for obvious solutions before more unusual diagnoses. Their teachers remind them that the less exotic option is generally the correct one. "When you hear hoof beats," they say, "think of horses, not zebras."

When people hear howling, they tend to think of wolves, not dogs. It is simply more exciting to have heard a *wolf* howling outside one's bedroom window than to have heard a dog, or to see a *wolf* not a dog by the freeway, or to have rescued a *wolf* than a dog. Everyone wants to be part of something special, and to see or touch a wolf is generally considered something special. People may be so eager to think that whatever is happening is something unusual and wonderful that they will grasp at any behavioral or physiological straw in order to label an animal "wolf"—just so it becomes a little more interesting to themselves and to others.

This is perfectly understandable behavior. Everyone wants to stand out from the crowd, and association with a wolf or wolf hybrid is a way to do that. However, this tendency must still be taken into account when evaluating an animal. Well-meaning people surrendering a pet or a stray may exaggerate an animal's history in the mistaken belief that such an exotic animal is sure to be found a good home, simply because it is so unusual.

In conclusion

While the mechanics of "wolf behavior," "dog behavior," and what happens when you get a wolf and a dog together seem, at first, to be quite simple, the reality is nearly impossibly convoluted. Simple genetics ("50%," "25%") is suddenly quite complicated when you realize that genes code for multiple traits, can be linked to one another and can affect one another, and that "wolf" and "dog" doesn't really mean much at the genetic level, since wolves and dogs are almost identical in a genetic sense. Other effects, such as misidentification of parent breed, unusual genetic "sports," or inbreeding, can confound the effect. Add to that the effects of nutrition, medication, or toxic compounds, and it becomes clear that so many factors affect the physiology of canid animals that it is very difficult to predict—especially from unknown ancestors as in the case of a rescued or stray dog—whether the animal is wolf or dog based solely on its physiology. Behavior is an equally complex minefield of conflicting influences which alter the behavior of dogs, wolves, and hybrids until one simply cannot be told from the other.

A number of factors—including shaking off excess water—can contribute to animals looking a little different than expected. Photo courtesy of Monty Sloan.

On the bright side, while factors in the environment can perform some major changes on an animal, there is a limit to how much the genetically coded appearance and behavior of an animal can be changed by environmental efforts. For example, hunting behavior, being such a valuable asset to a predator such as a dog or wolf, can often be difficult to fully sublimate through behavioral training. The pup that has been trained to not hunt cats may not be able to generalize non-hunting behavior toward guinea pigs or squirrels. Some individual dogs simply "do not have it in them" to develop guarding or attack behavior, no matter what training is used. Also, the older the dog and the more ingrained a behavior is, the harder it is to extinguish. In the end, no amount of nutritional supplements will induce a Chihuahua to grow to the size of a Great Dane, and no amount of training and socialization will induce a dog of any breed to fly.

Let us turn now to what we *can* know about the animals which arrive at shelters unnamed, unknown, and with no documentation.

Chapter 6
Practical Advice for Rescue Organizations and Shelters Working with Wolf Hybrids

It seems that the creation of a wolf hybrid can best be described as "a mess." Two closely related animals, which can be very difficult to tell apart either physically or genetically, breed. Their genes do a complicated little dance and assort themselves unpredictably, while environmental factors alter the expression of the genetic information. Then to top it all off, the parents may not be ideal, "textbook" ambassadors of their breeds, or may even be entirely different breeds than advertised. Behavior, of course, is all over the map.

Now that we have gained some insight on wolves and dogs and why they are so hard to tell apart, what do we do when we find ourselves saddled with something that we cannot easily identify as either? Though there is some advertising and the occasional news article claiming otherwise, there is as yet no definitive test, DNA or otherwise, which will reveal an animal's exact percentage of wolf content (please see Chapter 7 on DNA testing for further explanation). Even if there was such a test, knowledge of exact genetic wolf percentage does not necessarily usefully predict the *behavior* of the animal, which is what is most relevant to the rescue professional in any case. The goal in the evaluation of an animal by a rescue organization should primarily be to determine its *suitability as a household pet*. Its precise genetics may or may not even be relevant to this determination.

To this end we strive to offer a *practical* evaluation format which will allow persons to make some educated guesses about an animal submitted to them for identification. We must begin by, ironically, forgetting a lot of the things we know.

Discarding unhelpful labels: A wolf by any other name
"Fear makes the wolf bigger than he is." ~ German proverb

Any animal evaluation should begin with a clean slate, and that includes an attempt to cleanse ourselves of preconceived notions concerning the animal before us. Whether we are presented with an owner surrendering an aggressive "wolf hybrid" who has bitten a small child, or a nervous mother whose teenager has brought home a "wolf hybrid" puppy, our first aim, when considering such an animal, should be to put the word "wolf," and whatever positive or negative connotations it may have for us, as far from our heads as possible, whether it appears relevant or not. Starting from such a premise ("It's a wolf!") is counterproductive, and can actually affect one's image of the animal, possibly even more than the animal's actual physiology and behavior.

Even *thinking* the word "wolf" when working with an animal will cloud our judgment, affecting how we interact with the animal and how we interpret its responses to the environment, people, and other animals. Words can affect us even subconsciously. In his article "The Unbearable Automaticity of Being," Dr. John Bargh (who works in the delightfully named "ACME Lab" of Yale University) writes of an experiment in which human subjects were given "scrambled-sentence" tests in which they had to form coherent sentences from strings of apparently random words. In reality, the tests were seeded with specifically chosen "priming" words intended to bring out behavioral traits in the subjects. In one trial, the test was seeded with either belligerent words like "aggressive," "disturb," "rude," and "infringe" or with more passive words like "respect," "patiently," and "considerate." Subjects were then asked to walk to another room, encountering as they did so an investigator pretending to be a confused visitor, who was speaking to the examiner and blocking the subject's path. Sixty-seven percent of subjects exposed to the list of belligerent words interrupted the "visitor," whereas subjects exposed to emotionally neutral words interrupted the "visitor" 38 percent of the time. Subjects exposed to the passive test words interrupted the "visitor" only 16 percent of the time. In another trial, subjects exposed to words associated with age and the elderly ("Florida," "gray," "old") actually walked more slowly down the hallway leaving the exam room than did subjects exposed to neutral words!

Slapping the label "wolf" on an animal effectively primes people for encountering their preconceived notion of "wolf," whatever that may be. People who are *expecting* a vicious predator when interacting with an unknown animal will be more likely to interpret the animal's actions as predatory or dangerous. Thus their mental attitude about the animal will affect how they perceive their experience with it (Klaaren et al., 1994). Also, ironically, people who are afraid of wolves are more likely to react fearfully to animals presented as wolves, whether the animals are wolves or not, and the fearful behavior of the humans can even encourage fearful or possibly aggressive "wolf-like" behavior by the animal as it reacts to the human's apprehensive behaviors. That is, one can actually change the behavior of an animal through one's own behaviors.

For years, Wolf Park staff members have encouraged wolf sponsors who are meeting a wolf in person for the first time to think of the animal as an unfamiliar dog instead of a wolf. This causes the human to draw from their repertoire of "unfamiliar dog" greeting behavior—usually a much different, and much more confident, array of behavior than the array of behavior he or she would use if greeting a "wolf." Just changing the mental label on the animal changes how the person interprets its behavior and attitude, and how the person interacts with the animal.

Either way, the "wolf" label immediately attaches a lot of emotional baggage to a poor animal who has likely done nothing to deserve it. Refer to the animal as a "husky mix," or simply a "mixed breed." Call it a "dog," call it a "canid," or a "dog-oid," but allow the word "wolf" to slip quietly out the door for a moment. One can always bring it back again if it is needed in the future.

You're almost certainly looking at a dog

A good reason to consider all incoming canids "dogs" is that they very likely are. There is not a great deal of *data* on how many wolves and hybrids are actually kept by private owners in the United States and, mostly because of all the excitement mentioned in the preceding chapters, the available data is highly suspect. However, *based on our experience,* we offer the following thoughts concerning the relative likelihood of any given random animal being a dog, versus the same animal being a wolf.

According to the *U. S. Pet Ownership and Demographics Sourcebook* (2007 edition), compiled by the American Veterinary Medical Association, there are more than seventy-two million pet dogs in the United States. According to the U. S. Fish and Wildlife Service, in 2006 there were only 5,192 wild gray wolves in the lower forty-eight states, plus six to seven thousand in Alaska. This means there are *six thousand times* as many dogs as wild wolves in the United States. For every single wild wolf in the U. S., there are *six thousand* pet dogs. (And this data does not count feral, or stray, dogs, which may account for up to a million *more* animals (Coppinger and Coppinger, 2001)). Even if one counts the estimated sixty thousand wolves in Canada, that still leaves a respectable ratio of one thousand dogs (not including strays) to every wolf in North America.

The general consensus seems to be that there are around 300,000 (Willems, 1995) to 400,000 (Hope, 1994) wolf hybrids in the United States, although all sources we found seem to quote each other. Several papers note that "the USDA" made the original estimate of 300,000 animals. This appears to be directly traceable to the Willems article published in the *Animal Welfare Information Center* newsletter in 1995, which mentions the USDA coming up with the figure, but does not provide reference to where or how the UDSA might have obtained this number or how the data might have been collected. Remembering that this number is *highly* likely to be exaggerated, there are still approximately 180 times as many dogs as (almost certainly owner reported) wolf hybrids—again, not including feral populations of dogs in the calculation. It is still a good bet that any individual animal arriving in a shelter is not a hybrid, much less a wolf.

Getting a wolf out of the wild is harder than one might think. While tales abound of people—usually those living out in the country a hundred years or more ago—living seemingly almost arm-in-arm with wild wolves and regularly interbreeding their dogs with the wild packs, remember that these stories do not often originate with people whose primary desire was to be scientifically accurate. Even if one assumes there is truth to the old stories, it has been a long time since most people in North America lived in such solitude (and had such a luxury of time and resources) that they could pluck animals from the wild at will and raise them as pets. Since the passage of the Endangered Species Act in 1973, it has become much more difficult to take live wolves from the wild, since trade in endangered animals, including owning, trading, transporting, selling, or importing them from Canada into the Untied States, are all specifically prohibited by the Act. This does not prevent people from circumventing the law, of course, but it does make such activity much more difficult, and therefore less likely.

Recalling the behavior patterns of wild wolves, it would be highly inconvenient, if not downright unwise, to attempt to take an adult wild wolf into captivity with hopes of inserting it into a breeding program. Generally, the traditional method of taking a wolf from the wild involves taking pups from a den. This is harder than it sounds. As mentioned before, there really aren't that many wild wolves out there. Even in Canada, where there are sixty thousand wolves, those animals are spread out over four and a half million square miles with an average of one wolf per seventy-five square miles of land. A pack's territory may be more than three hundred square miles and their dens are not exactly marked with huge neon signs indicating their location. Wolves also regularly move their pups between dens, making it even less likely that someone will stumble upon a wolf den with pups in it (Paquet and Carbyn, 2003). While people have indeed taken wild wolf pups from dens—usually while the adults in the pack were being exterminated for "predator control" reasons—the likelihood of: a) finding a wild wolf den; b) happening to find that den filled with pups of just the right age; and c) getting a pup out of it and to one's house without incurring the wrath of either the adult wolves or the human authorities, is relatively small.

Beyond that, the wolf must reach breeding age (usually two years) and then actually reproduce in order to add its genes to the captive population. Throughout this book, we have presented some convincing evidence that wolves are at least a little more difficult to keep than a dog. While very young pups can be manageable, housebreaking problems, chewed furniture, destroyed architecture, a tendency to escape, and other issues mentioned previously generally preclude a wolf pup older than eight to twelve weeks from working out well in a human environment. As with all things, there are exceptions, but these cases are extremely rare. Because the behaviors generally exhibited by wolves are not usually what people are looking for in a household pet, "pet" wolves are very often euthanized (or "released into the wild" which, for a tame, hand-raised animal, generally amounts to the same thing) before they ever produce a litter.

In addition, as pointed out earlier, certain forces can cause people to over-represent the amount of wolf ancestry in an animal, knowingly or not. People are generally willing to pay more for an "exotic pet" than they are for a "plain old dog." There is, therefore, strong pressure for someone faced with an unwanted litter of mixed breed puppies to try to sell them as "wolf hybrids" rather than "mutts." Likewise, the "zebra effect" mentioned in the previous chapter can encourage some individuals to misrepresent their animals—consciously or unconsciously, both to themselves and to others—as having exotic ancestry increase their perceived value. Thus, of the canids claiming wolf descent, at least some (and likely a large percentage) will really be misrepresented dogs.

Lastly, while it is of course possible to keep a wolf as a pet, *most* people find keeping a wolf in a captive situation to be, at the least, highly inconvenient compared to keeping a dog. Most wolves who somehow end up as companion animals in human families are surrendered, abandoned, or euthanized long before they are able to produce litters. Breeders who do have actual wolves generally have to go to a lot of effort to keep them enclosed and find that they are great trouble to maintain compared to a dog.

We do not wish to impugn the heredity of the certainly handsome and beautiful representatives of real wolf heritage which do occur as pets. We have met several of them. As we have said before, people can and do keep wolves and hybrids as pets, and wolf hybrids are indeed out there. Our point here is not to say that no animal which comes into a shelter or rescue is ever a wolf. We wish only to suggest that, due to the above mentioned effects, any random canid "A" which enters a shelter or rescue is far more likely to be a dog than it is to be a wolf or a hybrid, simply because: a) dogs overwhelmingly outnumber wolves; b) there is such a huge tendency for people to over-represent the amount of wolf in their animals; and c) it is so difficult to really obtain and keep a wolf, for a breeding program or otherwise.

So, what can we actually say?
Our goal here is to prepare the reader for taking a look at an animal presented as a "wolf" or "wolf hybrid" in a new light, without all the preconceived notions we all get fed by media "experts," films, and literature, and with a new appreciation for how hybrids are created and what circumstances might have produced the animal at which they are looking.

We are not able, in this book, to give the reader the huge and varied background he or she will need to accurately identify an animal—no book can do that. We aim simply to guide the reader in their investigation of an unknown animal, and to point out ways in which such investigations commonly go wrong—usually, as we shall see, in identifying a wolf where one is not present. In the following section we will investigate a checklist of the common physical, behavioral, and background traits which can be assessed by a rescue professional, and explore to what extents these traits accurately suggest wolf or dog heredity.

Will we arrive at any definitive percentage of wolf ancestry? No. What we are doing here is looking at the animal's known behavior, looking at its physical properties, and making educated guesses about its future behavior based on its history and what we know of wolves, dogs, and hybrids. It does not matter, *practically*, whether the animal is actually genetically pure wolf or pure dog if it is displaying—or if its current behavior implies it is *likely* to display—behavior which makes it unsuitable for placement in an average home. It should not be adopted out, but instead be rehabilitated, sent to a suitable sanctuary, or humanely euthanized—whether it is genetically a dog, a wolf, or a kangaroo. If an animal of unknown heritage is displaying "doggy" behavior, suitable for a household pet, and appears, based on one's background knowledge and behavioral analysis to be likely to do so in the future, it should be treated as a dog (because it almost certainly is one) and given the same chance to find an adoptive home as any other dog.

With possibly inaccurate labels set aside, we now try to view our unknown animal with an open mind. Indicators of wolf or dog heritage can appear in two categories: physical and behavioral, with additional information coming from the *behavior history* of the animal. These three sources of information generally combine to form a much stronger picture of an animal than one source alone. We begin with the easiest evaluation, the physical, and of course with the problems that it has.

A wolf who looks like a dog, with a dog who looks like a wolf: Maggie and Abe, Mission: Wolf ambassador animals. Photo courtesy of Monty Sloan.

Physical evaluation

"Even the tiniest Poodle or Chihuahua is still a wolf at heart."
~ Dorothy Hinshaw Patent, author of "Dogs: The Wolf Within"

Since the advent of photography, it has been relatively easy to amass huge databases of photographs of different animals in order to demonstrate and compare anatomical features. A number of excellent handbooks have already been written—featuring extensive, detailed physical descriptions and a range of photographs—attempting to give people who have not worked with wolves an idea of what physical traits reveal the presence of wolf ancestry in an animal. Some wolf rescues have attempted to personally teach the staff of local dog shelters and rescues which traits to look for. Wolf Park regularly teaches behavioral seminars which expose participants to real, live wolves, up close. We find that, time and time again, even people who have been exposed to these excellent educational media continue to have difficulty discriminating animals with likely wolf heritage from unusually colored or shaped dogs. (The authors will agree that they, too, occasionally have such trouble.) It is impossible, unfortunately, to communicate a lifetime of viewing and comparing wolves, dogs, and hybrids through a single encounter with a wolf, or through a book. One can get the general idea, certainly, but until one actually encounters a variety of the animals, *correctly labeled*, one cannot really get a sense of what is what.

Wolves, for example, are often said to have "narrow chests" compared to dogs. Photographs demonstrate that this means that wolves' forelegs emerge from their bodies nearly touching at the top. The forelegs of dogs often emerge from their bodies with the width of a human hand, or more, between them. Big, muscular dogs may have a huge gap between the tops of their forelegs. However, as we have seen, dogs come in all shapes and sizes and even in broad-chested breeds there will be some individuals with narrower chests. This does not necessarily mean that they have wolf content. Instead, it means that the natural variation in the dog has produced an individual with a narrower chest than is considered standard for the breed. Also, "narrow" is a subjective term. A human who has worked a lot with Bulldogs and other "wide" breeds might consider the chest of a long, rangy breed like a Husky to be very narrow, while someone who works with wolves might consider the chest of a Husky to be quite wide.

Wolves have large heads for their body size compared to those of dogs. However, a breeder or fancier of Newfoundland dogs or Mastiffs, who have comparatively enormous heads, might consider a wolf's head to be comparatively small. Wolves have large paws for their body size compared to dogs. Not everyone agrees on the definition of "large paws." However, people who own Chihuahuas, for example, might think Huskies (who have very dainty feet compared to wolves) have large paws. There are also individual dogs who may have unusually large or small paws for their size. Wolves have straight tails, which do not curl up over their back. Many lines of captive wolves, however, simply because it is so difficult to obtain wild stock to expand the gene pool, and thus inbreeding occurs, display corkscrew or curly tails. It is not impossible that a pure wolf could have a corkscrew or curly tail. Some wild wolves have even been found with dewclaws on their hind legs (Ciucci, 2003), a trait which is primarily seen in dogs (Park, 2004), which is likely the result of a "doggy" ancestor or two in the *wolf* family tree (Randi, 2007). These animals have detectable dog ancestry, but that does not make them dogs in any practical sense, any more than detectable wolf ancestry makes a dog a wolf.

The "big head" of a pure wolf. Photo courtesy of Monty Sloan.

The "big head" of a Leonberger dog. Photo courtesy of Monty Sloan.

A pure wolf with unusually large (for a wolf) ears, which are also displayed by many of his immediate relatives. Photo courtesy of Monty Sloan.

Many individual dogs have been bred with golden-colored "wolf" eyes, even though they have no recent wolf heritage. What use is a checklist of specific characteristics when exceptions may be found for every single one?

An animal with a single wolf characteristic—an agouti (mottled black, brown, and white) color pattern, large paws, or golden eyes—is far more likely to be a dog with a single evolutionary "throwback" feature than it is to be a wolf masquerading as a dog. Real wolves, as we have seen, are hard to manage in captivity, and not all "wolves" and "wolf hybrids" being kept as pets are being correctly identified. *Many* dogs are not being correctly identified. There are far more "dogs that look like wolves" than real wolves existing in human hands. It is far, far more likely that any individual dog with one or two "wolfy" physical characteristics is simply dredging up something inherited from its distant ancestors than that it has recent wolf ancestry.

Physical evaluation checklist

Keeping in mind that everything is relative, we now take up the large list of traits which are used by experts to differentiate wolves and dogs. However, none of these traits is an absolute, and laypersons, whose experience has been primarily with one or two dog breeds (or one or two individual dogs), do not always find these landmarks easy to find, define, or use. We list some of the most common traits here, in order of ease of detection and relevance.

A pure wolf showing off many typical "wolf" characteristics. Photo courtesy of Monty Sloan.

"Dead giveaways" that the animal is highly likely to be a dog

- **Size:** Under 40 pounds
- **Coat pattern:** Multiple, large, bold spots like a Paint horse or a Dalmatian
- **Eyes:** Bright blue eyes, or one blue and one brown eye
- **Ears:** Floppy ears
- **Nose:** A pink nose, or pink skin around the eyes
- **Tail:** A *tightly* curled tail, or no tail at all
- **Legs:** Length less than half the length of the back.

Size. Typically animals with wolf heritage close enough in their ancestry to be of any significance are similar in size to wolves. It is not inconceivable that a very small, 65 pound wolf could be bred with an even smaller 30 to 40 pound dog to produce offspring that weigh less than half the typical median weight of an adult wolf. It is also possible that an abnormally large wolf could be bred with an atypically large dog such as a Mastiff to produce offspring that are behemoths compared to their wild ancestors. However, most animals with immediate wolf heritage will still be in the range of around 70 to 120 pounds with very few exceptions. (It sounds unlikely that someone would present a 30 to 40 pound dog as a pure wolf, but it has happened, personally, to one of the authors.)

Coat pattern. One of the first things that leads many individuals to suspect that an unidentified animal has wolf heritage is the most obvious trait of an animal: the coat color. We cannot stress enough that the "genetic lottery" can make for the possibility of any number of coat colors and markings in purebred dogs—including wolf-type markings. Agouti fur, a dark "saddle" marking down the back, or a dark spot on the tail over the post-caudal scent gland are all characteristics of wolves, but they are characteristics displayed relatively commonly by dogs as well. However, even an animal with all three traits is not necessarily a wolf. There are two coat patterns that wolves do not display which dogs do: large, bold spots like a Paint horse, or many tiny spots like a Dalmatian. Black wolves often have a *single* white spot on their chest or belly or toes, but none have so far been found with multiple large, white spots.

A piebald coat: almost certainly a dog. Photo courtesy of Monty Sloan.

Eyes. Wolves and dogs both display a fantastic array of eye color. Dogs, especially, have been bred to display every color—including the brilliant yellow most commonly associated with wolf eyes—so "yellow eyes" is not a giveaway trait. However, while the occasional wolf has shown up with very blue looking (usually really green) eyes, it is quite rare that an animal with immediate wolf heritage will have the classic baby blue, or bi-colored (one blue, one some other color) eyes commonly found in, for example, the Siberian Husky and the merle Border Collie. Blue eyes are a giveaway trait that an animal is very likely to be a dog. On the opposite side of the coin, brown eyes are not necessarily a sign that the animal is all dog. Although a wolf's eyes are not usually the rich, chocolate brown belonging to many dogs, their yellow-to-orange eye tones can sometimes darken and look brown, especially in photographs or in low light. Thus, brown eye color is not, in and of itself, an accurate indicator of dog ancestry, although it can be a good clue when combined with other traits.

Wolf eyes. Green eyes are rare in wolves, but it does happen. Photo courtesy of Monty Sloan.

Ears. Wolves have short, triangular, upright ears with fur inside them. Many people use the raw description that they look like the ears of German Shepherds. However, wolves have smaller, more triangular ears than the large, elongated ears of a typical German Shepherd. Note that the tips of the ears can be worn down by fly bites, bitten short by other dogs, or "trimmed" by frostbite, and the exact shape of the ears is not always a good indicator of ancestry. Wolves generally do not have floppy ears, except through damage or disease. An animal with naturally floppy ears, like those of a Labrador Retriever, is almost certainly a dog.

A wolf with typical small, furry ears. Photo courtesy of Monty Sloan.

Nose. Wolf noses and the skin around their eyes, even in pure white animals, are generally black or dark brown. An animal with a pink nose or eye-skin is very likely doggy, although pink noses can also result from illness or injury (such as sunburn). The coloration of other bare skin on the animal can help confirm if the pink nose is natural or the artifact of a physical condition. Pink skin (other than the inside of the mouth) is very uncommon in wolves.

A northern breed dog with a naturally pink nose. Photo courtesy of Monty Sloan.

Tail. A wolf tail is usually straight, although of course it can curl and bend while being "used." Keep in mind that the tails of Huskies and Malamutes curl tightly when they are raised over the back, but drape in a straight manner when relaxed and lowered. Wolf tails look the same when relaxed, but rarely form a full curl even when raised over the back. Permanent curls, twists, and abnormalities in the tail are not usually associated with wolf ancestry. A tightly curled tail makes it highly likely that the animal is a dog.

A Basenji, a dog breed with a naturally tightly curled tail. Photo courtesy of Lindy Ireland, through Flickr Creative Commons.

Legs. Wolves have very long legs, but so do many dog breeds. However, legs which are less than half the length of the back (think Basset or Dachshund) are likely to belong to a dog.

The very short, relative to body length, legs of a Basset Hound. Photo courtesy of Ethan Hall, genome.gov.

Less definitive indicators that the animal is likely to be a dog

- **Claws:** Clear or white-streaked toenails, dewclaws on the rear legs.
- **Chest:** Big, muscled chest like a bulldog.
- **Coat:** A thin, single-layered coat like a Greyhound.
- **No precaudal gland:** *Lack of* a gland about one third of the way down the top side of the tail.

Claws. Typically, wolves will have large, thick claws which are all black or mostly black. Streaking of white or clear coloration in the nails is usually a telltale sign that there is dog ancestry. However, individual variation does occur. There are purebred wolves that do not display all black toenails. It is also unusual (but not impossible) that an animal with recent wolf heritage would have dewclaws on the hind legs. (Most dogs, and virtually all wolves, do not have dewclaws on their hind legs. Hind leg dewclaws are primarily considered a "throwback" occurring in inbred, or line-bred, dogs.)

Chest. Wolves have a chest that is very laterally compressed (narrow). This is best viewed from the front while the animal is standing. In the case of a wolf, it should be difficult to get a flat hand (inserted fingers first) between the animal's forelegs. An animal with a big, muscular chest which easily accommodates a hand even while the animal is standing is probably mostly dog.

The narrow chest of a wolf. Photo courtesy of Monty Sloan.

Coat. Wolves have a "double layered" coat, as do many dog breeds. The coat consists of a dense, downy, insulating "fluff" layer right against the skin, and a layer of keratinized, rough "guard hairs" over that. It is unlikely that a suspect animal displaying only a single coat has close wolf ancestors. The concept of a double coat is very subjective, however, and in the summer, almost all dogs—and wolves—will appear to only have a single coat as most of the lower coat is shed out. Single-coated dogs include Greyhounds and Dachshunds. Double-coated dogs include Malamutes and Huskies.

No precaudal gland. Wolves possess a scent gland, called the precaudal or violet gland, about one third of the way down the top side of their tail (Busch 2007; Wilson, 1975). Its function is currently unknown. It appears in most wolves as a functional gland usually with a black marking over it in the fur. The gland is absent in many dogs, and therefore the lack of a black marking on the tail where the precaudal gland would be can be a strong suggestion that the animal has dog ancestry. However, some dogs, especially members of northern breeds, may still have vestigial markings or even glandular structures where the precaudal gland would be in a wolf.

The precaudal gland is visible as a dark spot on the top of the tail of this wolf. Photo courtesy of Monty Sloan.

Even less definitive indicators that mean the animal could be a dog

- **Facial markings:** Either dogs or wolves can have a "mask" over their eyes.
- **Paws:** Extremely "dainty" paws like a show-line Husky.
- **"Stop":** Wolves have less of a defined "stop" (bend where the muzzle meets the face) than most dogs, but this is a very ambiguous measure.

Facial markings. Many wild agouti-colored wolves have distinctive markings on their faces (pure black and pure white wolves, of course, lack these). Many different breeds of dog have retained similar facial markings to this day. Huskies and Malamutes, for example, have a number of highly distinctive masks and facial markings around the throat, face, cheeks, and eyes. These are very frequently mistaken for "wolfy" markings. These are fairly unreliable for determining ancestry.

A Czechoslovakian Wolf-Dog's facial markings. Photo courtesy of Monty Sloan.

A wolf's facial markings. Photo courtesy of Monty Sloan.

Paws. The paws on wolves are quite large relative to the body size of the animal. There are large-breed dogs with quite big feet, however, so this is not a definitive point. An animal with very "dainty" paws, like the feet of a show-line Husky or a Greyhound, which appear to be very small compared to the size of its legs, is likely to be mostly dog.

The paws of a wolf and a human. Photo courtesy of Monty Sloan.

"Stop." The stop (the point on the skull where the bridge of the muzzle meets the forehead between the eyes) has become very heavily pronounced in many breeds of dog as neotenic characteristics became more and more prevalent throughout several breeds. Typically, wolves have a longer, sloped stop rather than an abrupt, blocky stop where the slope of the nose seems to run into a road block where it hits the forehead.

A wolf with a very subtle stop. Photo courtesy of Monty Sloan.

A wolf with a more pronounced stop. Photo courtesy of Monty Sloan.

"Dead giveaways" that the animal is likely to be a wolf
There are none. For every physical trait exhibited by wolves, you will find a dog, if not an entire breed of dog, which displays it.

A note about puppies

It is very difficult to apply any of the above physical descriptors to young puppies—especially animals under four months old. Animals of almost every species grow in different ways. Just as human children hit growth spurts at different phases of their lives, and it is difficult to tell by looking at a one-year-old what they will look like when they are fifteen, it is difficult to say what a two-month-old puppy will look like once it hits sexual maturity. During the early months of an animal's life, colors in the fur change, the colors of the eyes may change, and different parts of the body (such as the head, legs, and paws, as discussed above) may seem (at least temporarily) to be grossly out of proportion simply due to normal patterns of growth in an animal. Thus, in a young, developing animal, the above mentioned physical attributes become *even less* reliable than they already are in adults, because they may change at any moment. Behavioral assessments are far more useful in puppies in gaining information about the animal.

Behavioral evaluation checklist

Now we turn to behavioral signs of ancestry, remembering that, since dogs are descended from wolves, they still display quite a lot of "wolf" behavior. The behavior has been sent through a funhouse mirror, but can still crop up in almost original form even in the most non-wolf-like dog.

As with the physical evaluation, the behavioral evaluation can be fraught with error, generally due to different standards on the part of every evaluator concerning what constitutes "shy," "friendly," "aggressive" behavior, or behavior resembling that of a wolf. These differing standards do not seem to be related to the amount of experience with or knowledge of animals (Tami and Gallagher, 2009), but may be more closely related to the observer's emotional state and/or personal feelings for the animal. Again, it is important to be as impartial as possible in evaluation and to remember that everyone's mileage may vary when it comes to even the definition of a behavior, let alone categorizing it as "wolf" or "dog" behavior.

"Dead giveaways" that the animal is highly likely to be a dog

Barking. Pure wolves very rarely bark, especially compared to dogs. Wolves only bring out their bark, which is an expression of terrible fear or arousal, for "special occasions." In contrast, dogs bark all the time—when excited, when stressed, when bored, when happy, or when defending territory. There are a few dog breeds (Malamutes and Huskies again) which rarely bark compared to other dogs, but they still bark more than wolves. An animal which barks a great deal (indeed, an animal which barks *at all*) is highly likely to be a dog.

In addition, the bark of a wolf, when it occurs, sounds quite different from the bark of a dog. The bark of a wolf is generally a low, breathy "wuuuuuuuf" sound rather than the "bowwowwowwow" bark of most dogs (Schassburger, 1978). Some breeds of dog

(Malamutes for example) can make this "wuuuuuf" sound when barking. However, the single, sharp "yap" bark of many dogs is extremely rare in wolves, and the "bow-wowwowwow" bark has not yet been documented in wolves.

Please note that the inverse of this statement ("It does not bark, so it must be a wolf") is not necessarily true. There *are* dog breeds which almost never bark (Basenjis come to mind). While an animal which barks a lot is not likely to have recent wolf ancestry, an animal which does not bark very often is not necessarily a wolf.

Less definitive indicators that the animal is likely to be a dog

Greeting. Generally, an animal that displays friendly behavior towards unfamiliar humans is a dog. Even the most highly socialized wolves tend to be reserved around unfamiliar humans in an unfamiliar space such as a shelter. An animal which comes barreling up to new people, smiling, wagging, and launching itself at their face to greet them is very likely to be a dog. (Again, the opposite is not necessarily true. Just because an animal is *not* thrilled to meet new people does not mean it is a wolf.)

A dog puppy gives a complete stranger an enthusiastic greeting. Photo courtesy of Monty Sloan.

Even *less* definitive indicators that mean the animal could be a dog

Training. Well-trained animals come from both species. An animal that appears to be well trained or know tricks is likely an animal which has spent a lot of time in human company. Purely through the fact that most people are likely to have more success training a dog than a wolf, an animal that appears to be well trained is probably more likely to be of more dog ancestry than wolf. There are, however, trained wolves out there, and one *can* train a wolf. This is not a definitive measure in itself.

An elderly, mellow wolf takes a walk with two familiar handlers and several unfamiliar visitors. This wolf is thoroughly socialized and well-trained, but he is still a wolf. Photo courtesy of Monty Sloan.

"Dead giveaways" that the animal is highly likely to be a wolf

Unusual destructiveness. We've all owned dogs who chewed shoes, rugs, and cords. This is natural canid curiosity, and both dogs and wolves show it. Wolves take destructiveness to a new level. Wolves can be an amazing destructive force in a human environment, however, producing chaos which will shock even experienced dog owners. If the animal is chewing chair legs, it could be either dog or wolf. If it is pulling down *walls and ceilings,* ripping all of a car's upholstery off, dismantling toilets, ripping kitchen cabinets off the walls, or shredding solid mahogany desks, it's very likely to have recent wolf ancestry.

The heavy, solid plastic "Boomer Ball"—reminiscent of a bowling ball—is one of few toys which will stand up to the undivided attention of a wolf. Photo courtesy of Monty Sloan.

Less definitive indicators that the animal is likely to be a wolf

Aloofness. This is defined as a low degree of interest in, or attachment to, humans. This differs from shyness in that the animal is not *afraid* of the human. Rather, it just could not care less that the human is around—unless the human is carrying food—and sometimes not even then. Very few dog breeds display this trait, since over the generations humans have tended to be more fond of dogs which display active interest in them rather than those who avoid them. However, working dog breeds (livestock guarding dogs and northern breed "sled" dogs, for example) have been created in which self-reliance and a not-entirely-full interest in humans are considered a virtue. In addition, wolves raised with intense human socialization can actually be more interested in humans than are some dogs (Udell et al., 2008). Also consider that an animal that may normally be highly interested in humans can come across as quite aloof when placed into an abnormal environment, such as a shelter. An aloof, disinterested attitude is not a *complete* marker that an animal has recent wolf ancestry, but it can be a part of the puzzle.

Even *less* definitive indicators that mean the animal could be a wolf

Shyness. Both dogs and wolves can be shy around new people. Extremely shy animals are often considered to be wolves or hybrids, simply because the people involved have never seen a dog display that degree of fear of humans. However, any dog can be just as fearful of people as a wolf, especially if the dog is feral or was raised in an impoverished environment and improperly socialized to humans. Shyness is not a reliable indicator of ancestry.

Howling. There are plenty of dog breeds that howl, from the obvious Huskies and Malamutes right down to the Chihuahua. Even if a breed doesn't normally howl, you will find individuals which do. Howling alone is not a good indicator of an animal's ancestry.

A wolf howling. Photo courtesy of Monty Sloan.

A Malamute howling. Photo courtesy of Julia Ballarin, through Flickr Creative Commons.

Digging or escaping. Any owner of a northern breed dog, or a high energy dog like a Border Collie, can show you fences their dog has been over, under, or through. Some dogs can open gate latches or even doors. The urge to get out and do something can be strong in a highly intelligent animal left alone at home with nothing to do, and this applies equally to both dogs and wolves.

Aggression. Those awesome movies with werewolves which come back to haunt people common misapprehension that wolves, when in the company of people, turn aggressive to defend themselves. Some do, but dogs also display aggression and often to a greater extent. Dogs generally have a lower fear of humans, so they are more likely to choose the "fight" option in a flight-or-fight situation. Most, but not all, wolves become relatively shy and nervous in captivity, demonstrating aggressive behavior only if cornered.

Behaviors are often just clues

Notice this comparatively large overlap in behavior. There are very few behaviors which offer any clearly definitive affinity for display in one species or the other. An individual behavior, taken by itself, may be displayed by either dog or wolf and offers no real clue as to the identity of an animal. Long-term observation of behavior *patterns*, however, *can* offer a clue, especially when taken in context of an animal's history and circumstances. Thus we turn for further information to the background evaluation, which hopefully will accompany the animal at intake.

Background evaluation

We reach now the third stage of our "bingo" game. Likely we have some "scores" at this point such as blue eyes, perhaps, or the knowledge that the animal has managed to chew its way right through the middle of a solid wood privacy fence. Now we put the final chips on the table by wrapping a behavior history around what we have gathered from physical evaluations.

Bingo? Photo courtesy of Monty Sloan.

When an animal is surrendered to a facility, generally an intake questionnaire is filled out or a brief interview conducted if possible, asking for at least the bare minimum of information. Sometimes many forms are filled out and fees are paid. Either way, there is an exchange of information, and there are some key questions to consider asking. Almost all of the "bingo scores" from the previous pages can be greatly augmented in their accuracy and relativity when historical patterns of behavior are known and can be factored into the assessment.

Initial intake information

It cannot be stressed enough that as much information as possible should be obtained from any previous owners/handlers of an animal at the time it is taken into an institution. This may sound obvious to some animal rescue personnel well versed in accepting surrendered animals, but it is especially important when accepting animals that are thought to have potential wolf origin. While all information should be taken with a grain of salt, information on the animal's behavior in situations which cannot be reproduced effectively onsite may become very helpful in making an overall determination about an animal. While we assume that any rescue organization already has a solid intake questionnaire in place, one can look below for a suggested list of topics the authors have found helpful when trying to identify an animal.

Sex, spay/neuter status. These are important data to have, since sterilization status and gender can so greatly influence behavior. Unneutered animals are far more likely to be "acting out" on hormone-influenced behavior such as roaming, dominance, and guarding, no matter what species they are. The gender of an animal can also affect how it interacts with humans and with other animals.

Date of birth/age. Wolves generally only become fertile once a year, during late February and early March, and therefore wolf pups are always born roughly in late April/early May. Dogs can come into season twice a year, any time of year, and may therefore be born at any time. An animal born in May is ambiguous. While wolf pups are usually born in May, of course dog pups can also be born in May. An animal born in January, however, is unlikely to have much recent wolf ancestry.

Age of an animal can affect its behavior and how it interacts with its environment. An elderly animal can tend to be mellow wherever it is, and may be less likely to challenge humans or dogs for dominance, or to chase small pets. Also, young puppies tend to be considered well behaved in any environment, simply because they are both physically incapable of causing significant damage to property or other pets, and because they are generally too young yet to feel a real need to defend their food or territory or challenge humans or other pets for dominance.

Why is the animal being surrendered? People turn in "wolves" for many different reasons. The circumstances surrounding an animal someone just found on the side of the road will be different from those of an animal who has been a pet for a long time. In the latter case, surrender may occur simply because a new neighbor told the owner that they have a hybrid. Frequently, it is because as the animal got older it became increasingly destructive or started to display aggressive behaviors toward its family, arousing suspicion it might be a wolf. The circumstances surrounding the surrender can help to describe the animal's previous life, and give some insight into both how much information the surrendering person has about the animal and how accurate it might be.

How long has the person surrendering the animal been in contact with it? It is useful to know how much experience the individual providing the information has had with the animal. There is beneficial information in knowing how long that person has had to assess the animal for themselves (i. e., did they just encounter it earlier that day or did they rescue it and keep it in their house for two weeks before bringing it to a shelter?). Someone who has encountered an animal daily for two weeks will have a better idea of what is "normal" behavior for that animal than someone who just scooped the animal up off the street.

Under what conditions did the animal live? Try to gather as much information about the animal's home life as possible, as this can shed light on a number of behavioral quirks. Some questions to ask may include:

- What, where, and how was the animal fed? By whom?
- Where did the animal sleep?
- How was it contained when outside? Was it allowed inside?
- How much time was spent with the animal?
- Which members of the family interacted with the animal?
- Were other pets present? What kind(s)?
- How was the animal disciplined, if at all?

As what breed is it being identified? Since this text is being consulted, it can be assumed that we are discussing animals that, somewhere down the line, have been identified as potentially being a wolf or a wolf hybrid. It may not be the person who is presenting the animal that gave the dog this appellation, however. Either way, the label the animal was wearing at the time ("dog," "wolf") can further enhance our ability to analyze situations being described. Remember that the label an animal has can affect how people act around it, as well as how they perceive its actions.

Who identified it as that breed? Was it the person bringing it in? The breeder? The previous owner? A veterinarian, a landlord, a police officer? A guy at a construction site? Once an animal obtains the label associating it with being a wolf, everyone down the line who handles the animal perceives it in a tainted light, so knowing the character and experience of the individual who *first* established the idea that the animal might not be a dog is important in helping determine how accurate that assessment was.

Name of breeder or likely breeder. In many cases, it will not be feasible to contact breeders or do extensive background checks, but knowing the original source of the animal ("I purchased it as a wolf hybrid from a recommended breeder" as opposed to, "The guy I got it from said it was part wolf.") helps to determine the likelihood of actual wolf ancestry as well as the accuracy of other data being received.

All data should be taken with a grain of salt, remembering how far and fast misinformation can travel, even unintentionally.

Further questions: Long-term behavioral indicators

These signs emerge only when looking at a long-term (more than three or four days) series of interactions, and can be gleaned only from those individuals who have spent some significant amount of time with the animals being surrendered.

Long-term indicators are generally only good in one direction: they are useful in implying that an animal is likely a dog. Both dogs and wolves freely demonstrate certain behaviors, such as chasing other pets as prey, but only dogs generally demonstrate the *lack* of those behaviors. Thus, the presence of the behavior, taken on its own, implies nothing, and an animal should not be considered a wolf just because it exhibits that behavior. The absence of a behavior, however, can imply a great deal about an animal, simply because wolves rarely lack that behavior.

Signs which can be reliable indicators

Interactions with children. This is a set of behaviors which cannot generally be tested in an institutional setting. For a great many obvious reasons, there are not a lot of parents willing to volunteer their young children as test subjects for assessing the behavior of an unknown animal.

It is more likely that an animal with recent wolf ancestry will not interact well with very young children (ages five and under). As mentioned earlier, wolves typically find little difference between the actions and vocalizations of small children and those of distressed prey. These animals do not exhibit submissive greeting behavior to human children; instead they adopt an intensely interested stare and sometimes attempt to grab the child and take it away. On the other hand, an animal with a history of positive interactions with children—friendly, submissive greeting, rolling over, and showing the belly—is typically less likely to have direct wolf ancestry.

Note should be taken of the ages of the children with which the animal has been observed. As children grow, they become more similar to adult humans and less similar to prey. An animal which did fine with a house full of teenagers may not be similarly tolerant if presented with toddlers.

We remind the reader to recall, when hearing testimony concerning behavior toward children, that people can mistake predatory behavior for friendly interest. Predatory behavior, which includes stalking with a relaxed face, wide open eyes, and forward facing ears, can look like general interest, especially to someone who still subscribes to the "old documentary" theory that wolf hunts involve a lot of growling and snapping. In fact, hunting wolves can look quite happy, including panting and sometimes wagging tails, which should be taken into account when hearing a surrendering owner mention how much Duke took a polite interest in little Bobby. (Wolf Park has had as part of its educational programs, for more than twenty-five years, a presentation wherein two to four wolves are introduced to a herd of healthy American bison in a large open field. The bison, weighing ten times as much as the wolves, have little to fear, but visitors can observe the interplay of predator and prey and observe real hunting behavior as well as real—and extremely effective—anti-predator measures on the part of the bison. A number of visitors express surprise at the calm, seemingly non-aggressive, attitude of the wolves during this event.)

Hunting wolves, with typical expressions: "Oh boy, oh boy, oh boy...!" Photo courtesy of Monty Sloan.

As we noted in earlier chapters, some wolves do regard human children as pups, and so this is not a definitive pointer one way or the other. Also, wolves grow and learn throughout their lives, and even a wolf who grew up treating children as puppies may later change his mind when he sees one acting like prey. However, in general, a lot of predatory behavior towards children or other persons (notably the handicapped or the elderly) who do not move like normal adult humans is a strong sign of wolf ancestry or a sign of an unusually highly motivated hunting dog. Either way, you are unlikely to want this animal in your house.

Note that an animal with a low instance of positive interaction with human children is not necessarily a wolf. It should be reiterated here that *all predators*, including domestic dogs of all breeds, *are capable of injuring or killing children*. Dog breeds from Beagles to Cocker Spaniels have bitten humans, including children. However, a wolf is much, much more likely to immediately *view children as prey* than is a dog. Most dogs do not view human children as food items.

Interactions with other canines. This can usually be assessed more readily than interactions with children in an institutional setting. If a facility does not already have a set of protocols for testing a dog for compatibility with other dogs, we recommend that they contact someone with experience before attempting to do so. It can be described to the utmost detail in writing, but formal dog-to-dog assessments should be supervised in person by someone with extensive experience in the matter.

Aggression toward other canines is not a strong determining factor in assessing probable ancestry. Both dogs and wolves run the gamut from shy and docile to aggressive and dominant. However, it can be a good indicator in that an animal which lacked dog-to-dog aggression, and got along well with every dog it met, would be much more likely to be a dog. A notable exception to this would be an immature animal as juvenile wolves and dogs both tend to automatically submit to, and get along with, older animals.

Interactions with other pets. Again, this is a situation that can be difficult to test in an institutional setting. Because of the wolf's tendency to view small, wriggling things as interesting and edible, animals with recent wolf ancestry will typically display a high degree of predatory behavior towards other pets, especially small pets. Of course, there are plenty of dog breeds which also still have the prey drive in sufficient amounts.

Where this indicator comes in handy is in its inverse; an animal which does well with cats, rats, hamsters, chickens, and other small pets, and doesn't seem to have had a predatory thought come into its head during the time it has spent with those animals, is very likely to be a dog.

It took years of intense socialization for this wolf to reach this level of happy, calm interaction with humans. Photo by Jessica Addams.

Interactions with adult humans. A long (the longer, the better) history of happy, friendly, fearless interactions with dozens of new humans, often in new and unusual (to the animal) locations, generally indicates an animal which is very, very likely to be a dog. Animals with close wolf ancestry are likely to demonstrate less, if any, friendliness to strangers.

Wolves are not born with a genetic predisposition for close contact with humans. As such, a wolf that did not experience extensive socialization during its first few months of life may be very shy, nervous, or even overtly aggressive in its fearfulness of people.

Though we have met some wolves who were quite friendly with multiple strangers *when in a familiar setting*, even a very well-trained and well-socialized wolf with a lot of human interaction in its background is very likely to become nervous or shy in new locations and without the backup of a familiar human friend.

Of course, dogs can also display fearful behavior in new spaces. "Shyness" is not a trait solely exhibited by wolves. "Shyness" should thus not automatically disqualify an animal from being considered a dog, although "extreme friendliness" in multiple unfamiliar situations just about clinches the animal *not* being a wolf.

Guarding behavior. Wolves are much more likely to have problems in this category. It is, after all, completely natural for a wolf to defend what resources it has obtained, and it generally devotes much more energy to this than will a dog. However, many dogs also demonstrate problems with food and resource guarding; one of the author's families once owned a ten-pound Lhasa Apso which aggressively defended items, to the point of eventually outright attacking its owners. Again, this sign is most useful in its inverse: an animal which does not guard food, toys, or other resources is more likely to be a dog.

Signs which are more ambiguous indicators

Trainability. It is commonly thought that wolves are difficult to train. This is both right and wrong at the same time. Wolves are phenomenally intelligent animals with a vast capacity for learning. However, much of their genetic pre-programming embeds very strongly many of the behavior patterns that they have established during infancy (such as hunting for prey, territorial and food defense, etc.). This makes these behaviors very hard to remove or alter simply by training, especially when compared to dogs.

This difficulty is compounded by the fact that wolves usually have no built-in drive to pay any attention to humans whatsoever, much less perform actions from which they cannot see a direct benefit to themselves. They learn just fine; the trick is getting them to learn what you want to teach them. The people who think you cannot train a wolf are quite accurate in the sense that it is much more difficult to find convenient, easy, simple ways to motivate a wolf to do what you want than it is to find ways to motivate a dog.

Dog trainer Ken McCort target training two wolves. Wolves are eminently trainable, provided their motivation is sufficient. Photo courtesy of Monty Sloan.

Lack of responsiveness to motivators like praise or petting, or lack of interest in training, are generally not good factors to use in trying to assess the ancestry of an animal. There are many dogs, Huskies for example, which are difficult to motivate, and adopt a notorious "couldn't care less" attitude during training sessions. (In fact, one of the author's families once owned a Miniature Schnauzer with a similar problem.)

Sexual cycle. Female wolves come into estrous only once a year, generally in late winter, when the amount of light each day begins to increase (Walker, 2000; Peterson, 1984; Bissonette, 1936). Likewise, affected by photoperiod (the relative length of daylight at a given time of year), the males are fertile for only a small period of the year, overlapping the female's estrous. A dog's sexual cycles is not as affected by photoperiod as is that of a wolf (Crockford, 2000). Female dogs can come into estrous at any time, and males are fertile year round (Jochle and Andersen, 1977). While having only a single estrous per year during late winter is a strong sign of wolf ancestry, this must be included in the "ambiguous" headings; most rescue animals will not, for various reasons, have the option to display the full extent of their instinctive sexual behaviors. Also, many owners may not have kept accurate records of estrous cycles, and it requires active attention to tell if a male is fertile or not. Only one breed of dog, the Basenji, has a single annual estrous whose timing is controlled by photoperiod (Fuller, 1956).

This background information contains some of the most important things that can be learned about an animal. Present behavior is one thing; a long-term history of behavior *patterns* is far more useful, and will help most in determining what kind of behavior the animal is likely to display in the future.

Behavior over ancestry: What we can infer from our assessments

What we now have in our hands is an animal and hopefully multiple consistent scores—such as "blue eyes," "a pink nose," and "very friendly greeting behavior towards unfamiliar humans" or "no especially doggy characteristics," "aloof behavior," and a "long history of predatory behavior toward small animals" which describe it.

Overwhelmingly, it will be possible to see a preponderance of scores pointing at one decision or the other. "It doesn't bark; it only howls" is a single score signifying, by itself, very little. Plenty of northern breed dogs bark relatively rarely, and it's possible for a dog owner to have never heard his or her animal bark. However, "doesn't bark" coupled with "aloof attitude" coupled with "predatory behavior" coupled with "damaging fights with other dogs" coupled with "destroyed a couch" coupled with "yellow eyes, a long, straight tail, and large paws," starts to form a strong case for an animal *which is not necessarily a wolf*, but which is displaying very wolf-like characteristics, and either needs to be placed with a specialized sanctuary or a very carefully chosen home, with people experienced with "high maintenance" animals. (Even with a behavior history like that, he can still make *someone* a good pet. It's just harder to find that someone.)

All dog (German Shepherd)—but not every household is ready for this high-energy, strongly focused, intelligent animal. Photo courtesy of Monty Sloan.

Note that the above scores could also describe a purebred Malamute (or Husky, or German Shepherd, or….). So what are we learning from this? We are learning that a practical animal evaluation is used to determine *the likely course of potential future behavior* rather than ancestry. Actual genetic makeup of the animal is irrelevant. Our hypothetical Malamute described above would be *genetically* 100% dog, but look at that behavior history: "aloof attitude; predatory behavior; fights with other dogs; destroys furniture." Or regardless of his ancestry, he's racking up points on the, "I'm not going to be a good pet for the average person" scale. *We don't have to call him a wolf to choose not to place him in a home.* We don't have to euthanize him in a panic because he's got "wolf ancestry" or because he's displaying those "wolfy" behaviors. We don't have to bring wolves into the equation at all. He's still a dog: he's just displaying behavior most people probably don't want in a pet.

Looks like a wolf, but the behavior is all dog. Photo courtesy of Ryan Talbot.

Likewise, we could get scores like "great with kids," "no detectable predatory behavior," "trains easily," and "has been owned by a family for 10 years." Whether the animal is genetically a dog or a wolf, an animal displaying this kind of behavior would likely be a good pet for someone and should be considered for adoption. Here is the animal we want to save even if he might be a wolf because he has "yellow eyes," a "narrow chest," "long legs," and a "straight tail." Despite that, his behavior score: "Great pet!" He looks like a wolf, but he's almost certainly genetically a dog. Remember, there are between one and six *thousand times* more dogs than wolves out there, there are many reasons a dog may look just like a wolf, and lots of circumstances conspire to encourage a perception that there are more wolves and hybrids out there than there actually are. Until we have some accurate, convenient, inexpensive, and *practical* measure by which to differentiate "wolf" from "dog" it is more useful to everyone, especially this poor animal, to call him a dog, because *he is acting like a dog*.

If only we had such a method! Here is where a lot of people start to think about DNA testing. Unfortunately, while DNA testing has the potential to eventually be used for accurate identification of animals, so far the science has not yet progressed far enough to live up to its promises. DNA testing is not (yet) accurate, convenient, inexpensive, or practical. . . although we have high hopes it eventually will be.

CHAPTER 7
The Current State of DNA Testing

Note: Some of the material in the first part of this chapter is quite technical and beyond what the reader may want to attempt to learn. We provide it, however, because the issue of what a DNA test can and cannot do is important to know as testing becomes more widespread. In addition, DNA research continues to evolve and significant advances are likely to occur in the coming years.

In recent years, there has been a growing interest in how science might aid in differentiating dogs (and other canids) from wolves in a more definitive fashion than is possible at present. Skull morphology assessments (Iljin, 1941) are relatively accurate, although not infallible, but they are not much use to the shelter worker, as the animal generally must not be using its skull at the time of measurement. Interest has thus ranged to other methods of identification, especially that of DNA testing. Much ado has been made recently about various DNA tests which purport to identify which breeds of dog have produced a mutt, and some of which claim to be able to identify wolf hybrids, apparently on the basis of their DNA not matching that of any other dog breed.

Unfortunately, DNA testing has not yet advanced to the stage it has in the movies, where one stuffs a test tube into the side of a computer and computer-generated DNA helices form on the screen, merge, and start flashing under the blinking word "MATCH." A strand of DNA is billions of molecules long, and it would take a dedicated, high-speed computer days (if not weeks) to read the entire thing and then further time to compare and match it to a similar strand. This may theoretically be possible even now, but at the moment that kind of DNA testing is still hardly efficient with regards to time.

DNA testing now

"DNA is an abbreviation for deoxyribonucleicantidisestablishmentarianism, a complex string of syllables." ~ Dave Barry

We feel we should note that the following explanation has been massively simplified. For clarity, we're only going to be looking at one half of the DNA molecule. The DNA molecule is actually formed by two long strands wound around each other, so each adenine "A" molecule is really matched by a thymine "T" molecule on the other strand of the double helix, so instead of the code "reading" "AAA," as described below, we're really looking at a connected string of "AT" "AT" "AT" pairs. However, a complete explanation of DNA is beyond the scope of this book. For a more in-depth understanding of DNA structure and how the DNA molecule is put together, duplicates, stores information, and is "read" into proteins, please see one of our favorite books: *The Cartoon Guide to Genetics*, by Larry Gonick.

Since we cannot (yet) match whole strands of DNA to each other like they do in the movies (and, in any case, the actual physical difference between two strands of DNA from the same species—humans, for example—may be as little as 0.1%), what we *can* do is select certain known *markers* (static locations in a DNA strand that are selected for comparison) and examine how they vary from individual to individual. Common DNA tests compare the *sizes* of *pieces* of DNA cut out of the whole strand.

The most common marker used in DNA testing today is *the short tandem repeat*, or STR (occasionally known as the variable number tandem repeat, or VNTR). The DNA "code" is made up of the pattern in which molecules of adenine, guanine, cytosine, and thymine—represented by the letters A, G, C and T respectively—appear in the strand of DNA. For example, part of the DNA code where six adenine molecules appear in a string might be represented by "AAAAAA," and one where cytosine and thymine molecules alternate would be represented by "CTCTCT." An actual string of DNA is made up of several *billion* molecules ("ACCTCGAGCTAGGATCGAATC-GATCGAGTCGATCTA ATCGATCGGATCGACCTAGCTAGCT…") and could not possibly be reproduced in this book.

Every individual has several different locations in their DNA where a little part of the DNA code repeats itself several times. These are STR locations, or *loci*. The true function of these STR loci is not fully understood, but, as the number of repeats in each STR is heritable, and varies from person to person (and from dog to dog and wolf to wolf), it is possible to use differences in the length of these STR loci to identify relationships between individuals.

For example, consider a hypothetical locus—we'll call it the IM, for "imaginary," locus. Our imaginary IM locus is formed of a variable number of repeats of the sequence AT (an adenine molecule followed by a thymine molecule). Sometimes, the IM locus has four repeats of the adenine-thymine AT sequence: ATATATAT. Sometimes, the IM locus has fifteen repeats of the AT sequence: ATATATATATATATATATATATATATATAT.

If you consider that each "A" and each "T" is really an adenine or a thymine molecule, you can see that a string of four repeats (ATATATAT) has eight molecules in it, and would have less *mass* (be smaller) than a string of fifteen repeats, which would have thirty molecules in it. If you could *isolate* the IM locus (snip it out of its surrounding DNA strand) from two individuals, and somehow weigh the DNA making up each locus, you could compare the weights of the two DNA strands to see if they had the same weight, e.g., the same number of repeats at the IM locus.

Scientists *can* snip out just a single STR locus from a strand of DNA, and that's how they do DNA testing. First, they identify the locus that they wish to snip out, and map the surrounding DNA. Since only 0.1% of DNA changes from individual to individual, the STR loci are nearly always bordered by identifiable bits of DNA that do not usually change. Scientists use man-made snippets of DNA called *primers*, which locate and bind to known sequences of DNA that border the STR locus, to essentially cut the STR sequence out of the DNA strand, so it is floating by itself and can be analyzed.

A single DNA strand is very small. In order to make it easier to see and analyze, scientists perform a *polymerase chain reaction* (PCR) on the snipped-out STR locus, making hundreds of billions of copies of it, so there is enough material to be seen by the naked eye, or at least by the equipment running the test. Once there are enough copies of the DNA strand to be used, it is run through a gel through which different sizes of molecule move at differing speeds. (The process is called *gel electrophoresis*, and it can get a little complicated, but basically an electrical field draws the DNA molecules, which are ordinarily negatively charged, through the gel, from top to bottom.) Because of the gel's resistance, bigger molecules move more slowly than smaller molecules through the gel. (Imagine skydivers with parachutes of different sizes. Bigger parachutes will catch more air as they fall, and take longer to reach the ground. Smaller parachutes will encounter less air resistance, and will reach the ground more quickly.) This separates DNA strands of various sizes. In this way, one can tell how the length of the STR strand of one particular person compares to the length of the STR strand of another person.

For example, our fictional IM locus has two alleles (remember, an allele is a variation of the same gene, or in this case different versions of the same STR): one with four repeats, and one with fifteen repeats. If you snip a copy of each allele out, and run it down the gel, the DNA strand with four repeats will be smaller than the DNA strand with fifteen repeats and will move much further down the gel. If you cut the IM locus out of the DNA of two individuals and run the results through the gel, you will see bands (or bars, or peaks, depending on exactly which test you run) indicating the relative mass of each individual's IM locus. If they both have the same number of repeats at the IM locus, their bars will appear at about the same distance down the gel. If one individual's IM locus is larger (has more repeats), their DNA strand will not travel as far down the gel as the smaller DNA strand.

7 — THE CURRENT STATE OF DNA TESTING

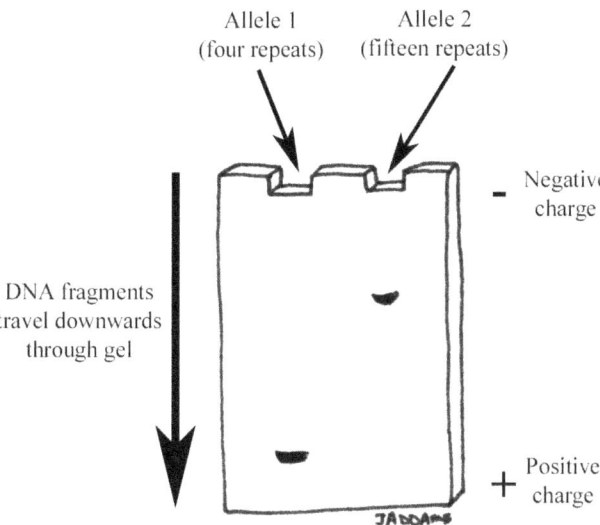

The DNA of the individual with the four-repeat allele travels much further than the DNA with the fifteen-repeat allele. The smaller molecule, with only four repeats, can move further against the resistance of the gel.

To complicate matters, everyone has *two* copies of every locus—one from their mother, and one from their father. This can result in offspring who carry two different copies of a certain locus. Both loci will show up on the results, and the offspring can be matched to its parents. For example:

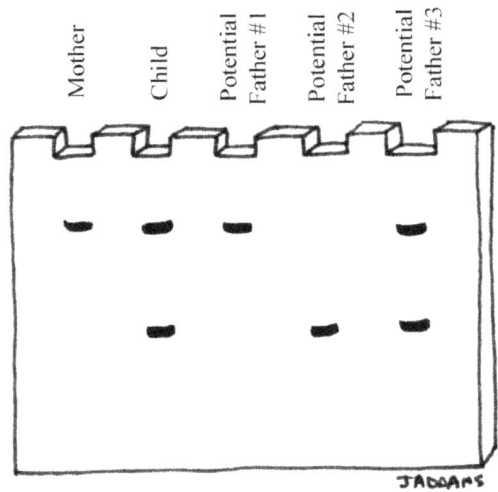

Gel Analysis of the IM Locus in five individuals

The mother in this hypothetical example has a large number of repeats in her IM locus (see how her DNA strand did not make it very far down the gel). Her offspring has two bars—one high, meaning it was a heavy strand of DNA, and one low, a light strand of DNA which traveled further than the first. Her child therefore has two copies of the IM locus—one from the mother and one from the father, each with a different allele. The allele with more repeats (the top bar) likely came from the mother, but the mother could not have provided a copy of the allele with only four repeats, as she does not have one herself. Therefore, the other allele likely came from the father. Potential father #1 has two identical IM alleles, both coding for fifteen repeats. He could not have provided the allele with only four repeats to the child. Candidate #1 is therefore definitely not the father. Potential father #2 has two identical IM alleles, both coding for four repeats (see how far the smaller DNA strands have traveled?). He could well have provided the other allele to the child. So could potential father #3, who, like the child, has a copy of each allele.

Of course, one locus may not vary much between individuals, especially in a population of closely related individuals. To maximize the effectiveness of DNA analysis, scientists usually look at several different STR loci at once when they compare one individual's DNA to another's. Most in-home dog DNA tests compare anywhere from one hundred to four hundred loci. Once again, the complication of this matter is part of the point. We're merely looking at a single locus in the examples above. Imagine looking at several hundred at once!

Applying DNA testing to canids

Because we cannot simply "read" the DNA strand end to end (not yet, anyway), all we can do is examine variations at known loci and compare one strand to another. How is this used to identify, for example, the ancestral breeds involved in the formation of a mixed-breed dog?

First, one must build up a database of known DNA—that is, strands taken from animals of known breeds, like Labrador Retrievers, German Shepherds, or Siberian Huskies. Since there is considerable individual variation even within a breed, the more individual strands are in this database, the better. For each breed, data must be taken down about as many markers, or STR loci, as possible. The more individual spots on a DNA strand we can compare, the more likely we will be able to identify similarities and differences between two animals. (How would you tell a cat from an owl if you could only look at the color of their eyes to tell them apart? You would have a better picture if you could also look at the number of legs they have, whether they have a muzzle or a beak, external ears, etc.)

Once you have a database of known individuals, you can start to compare unknown individuals to that database and see if they resemble any of the known individuals. For example, let's say we have a database of information about three loci, A, B, and C, and breed information about Labradors, Shepherds, and Huskies.

Labradors have a small number of repeats at locus A, a medium number at locus B, and a large number at locus C. Shepherds have a medium number of repeats at all three loci. Huskies have a large number of repeats at locus A, a medium number at locus B, and a small number of repeats at locus C. Remember that having more repeats at a locus means that the sample will travel a shorter distance on a gel. Running the dogs' DNA through gel electrophoresis would look like this:

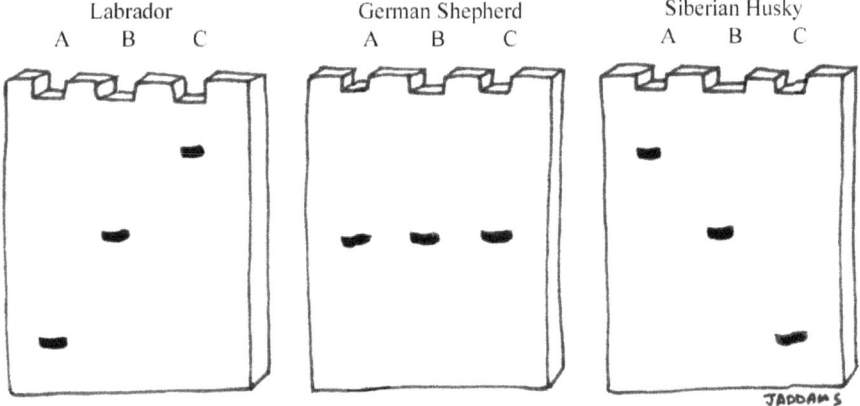

Imagine comparing these three breeds only on the basis of locus B. They are all identical. The more loci one uses, the better a picture one obtains.

Compare these three breeds now to theoretical unknown individuals X and Y:

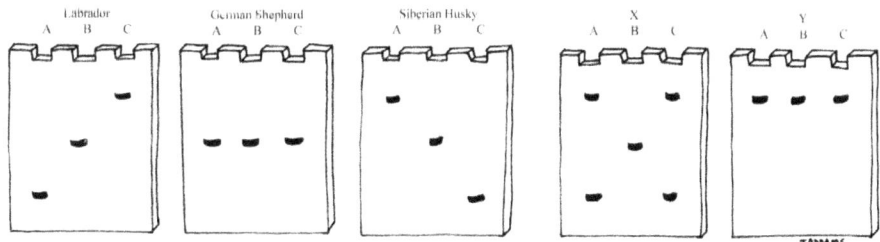

What can we say about individual X? X appears to have *both* large and small numbers of repeats at loci A and C, and a medium number of repeats at locus B. Remembering that individual X inherited two copies of each locus, one from each parent, individual X is likely to be a Labrador/Husky cross, as its decoded DNA shows similarities to both Labrador and Husky, and less similarity to German Shepherds.

Of course, there are more than three breeds of dog in the world, and purebreds are not the only animals to reproduce. Individual Y is something of a mystery. It appears to have large numbers of repeats at all three loci. None of the other breeds look like that. Is Y a mix with a breed not in our database? Two breeds? Is it a spontaneous mutation (not likely with two loci simultaneously, but not impossible)? All we can say about Y, from the information we have, is that Y is probably not a Labrador, a Shepherd, or a Husky.

The Metamorphix web page states, "If your pet's breed composition contains non-validated breed(s) the test may identify [other, validated] breed(s) earlier in your dog's ancestry." This means that sometimes the DNA tests fail—when your dog is a "non-validated breed," for example—or report false positives. In this way the offspring of a Collie/Schnauzer mix mated with an American Pit Bull Terrier—a breed not currently recognized by the AKC, and therefore not recognized by most testing laboratories which base their breed lists on those recognized by the AKC—would likely be identified by the test solely as a Collie/Schnauzer mix, because the laboratory would not have background data to identify the American Pit Bull Terrier DNA.

Some people would have one believe that the fact that individual Y's DNA does not match any of the known samples means individual Y is a wolf, but the animal could just as easily be a mix of several breeds, or even just a breed not yet in the database. Just because Y is not any of the breeds in our database does not mean that it must be a wolf.

A brief note on mtDNA and Y-DNA

So far, we have only dealt with the DNA found in the nucleus of the cell. This is the most common type of DNA, and is simply referred to as "nuclear" DNA.

A couple of other "flavors" of DNA are of particular use to geneticists, and may crop up in conversations about heredity. Species with genders have special chromosomes which determine the gender of the developing embryo. The female has two copies of the "X" sex chromosome and the male (under normal circumstances) has one "X" and one "Y" chromosome. The X and Y split during meiosis, so each sperm carries either an X or a Y chromosome; which sex chromosome is carried by the fertilizing sperm determines the sex of the embryo. Since DNA on the Y chromosome, or Y-DNA, can only come from a male parent, it can be useful for determining lineages and following the pattern of gene transmission through a pedigree. Y-DNA is also nuclear DNA, since the Y chromosome (along with the X) is found in the nucleus.

DNA is not, however, found exclusively in the cell nucleus. Organelles (tiny individual structures contained within the cell) called mitochondria—little "energy factories" for a cell—also contain DNA. The mitochondrial DNA, or mtDNA, molecular strand is much shorter than that of nuclear DNA, and instead of being the familiar "X" shape of supercoiled nuclear DNA, mtDNA's molecule is shaped in a circle like a donut. Sperm are too small to contain mitochondria, so all mitochondrial DNA comes from the egg, provided by the mother. Thus mtDNA can be used to trace maternal lineages. Also, since mtDNA does not split and re-assort during meiosis, it does not change as much between individuals as the nuclear DNA. It can be used to follow pedigrees over hundreds of thousands of years, and to measure the process of evolutionary change.

Since researchers are interested right now in how wolves and dogs evolved, much has been made in the news of mtDNA testing in both species. However, the scientists are studying patterns of gene expression and inheritance; they are not keeping a database of which genes are "wolf" and which are "dog" (and, in fact, they are discovering more and more that wolves have a number of "dog" genes, and vice versa). Data currently being gleaned from examination of mtDNA is more useful in the study of evolutionary patterns than in detection of wolf ancestry in an individual. While the study of mtDNA has revealed a lot about how dogs and wolves are related, mtDNA genotyping is still done the same way as genotyping performed with nuclear DNA, and suffers from the same flaws. It still has not reached a state of relevance, convenience, and efficiency for the shelter or rescue.

Current tests have unfortunate flaws

The commercially available "doggie DNA" tests are just fine as entertainment-quality "research" goes, but they should be considered unreliable for something as delicate as determining breed in, for example, a legal case.

First, their databases are very new—the companies are only a few years old and cannot possibly have built up sufficient background information to be able to identify "any" breed. The Mars WisdomPanel MX Mixed Breed Analysis test has, according to its web site, data from "130" AKC registered breeds— but how many individuals of each breed did it evaluate? The site claims that over thirteen thousand samples were collected. If the database represents 130 breeds of dogs, that means only one hundred samples were collected for each breed. What about the approximately fifteen percent of AKC breeds (as listed on its web site) for which it has no data? What about the breeds that the AKC does not recognize? Other tests use a database of only one hundred breeds. The AKC currently registers (according to its web site) more than 160 breeds, and overseas breed registries recognize four hundred or more breeds.

Second, the databases rely—not always entirely, but at least partially—on *owner identification* to determine the breeds of their "baseline" dogs. As we have seen, dog genetics is not always an exact science, and not every owner is equally reliable when it comes to properly identifying even a purebred dog. One of the labs whose sites we viewed, in early 2008, was actively soliciting DNA from owners with whom it had no relationship. If someone sent a Labrador sample in and labeled it as being from a German Shepherd, how would that facility know? (By the time of publication, however, that site no longer solicited DNA samples.) Other sites use AKC registration to determine the ancestry of a dog. AKC registration takes place without the dog, or its sire and dam, necessarily being viewed by anyone other than the owner; it can take place entirely online. There is not yet a database in existence with a *large* number of *reliably identified* samples representing all, or even nearly all, dog breeds.

The best we can do, DNA-wise, at this time is to identify "markers" (the individual STR loci) in populations of genetically similar individuals and be able to tell, from the presence or absence of those markers in a sample, if an unknown individual has DNA which closely resembles that of our known bloodline. Genetic testing can indicate that an unknown individual animal is, or is not, related to wolves in an area provided the local wolf population has been genetically studied, but if the unknown individual is simply from another population of wolves and has either migrated or escaped from captivity into the wild, its DNA will not show up with some mystical "wolf" stamp. It will only show up as not related to the native population. A feral mixed-breed dog, or a wolf hybrid, would produce similar results in such a test.

Even were the above problems solved, the unfortunate issue of budget remains. Current DNA tests for dogs cost upwards of one hundred dollars per animal—hardly an efficient use of resources for a non-profit organization.

Present day research

Many researchers are currently at work studying the DNA of wolves and dogs. These studies are unfortunately somewhat limited in scope (and availability) to be of practical use, at this time, to a rescue professional in identification of wolf hybrids.

One problem is that of scale: Few researchers (indeed, few people of any sort) have access to a large population of wolves. Most current DNA studies—in fact, most wolf studies in general—involve a database of 150 or fewer individuals (for example, Fatjó et al., 2007; Kyle, 2006; Vilà and Wayne, 1997; Laikre, 1992; MacDonald and Ginsburg, 1981) this is less than one quarter of one percent of the North American population of wolves, and generally all the wolves in a study come from the same facility or geographic area and are somewhat closely related to each other. Along with this tiny sample of individuals, sometimes the target study area of the DNA itself is minute. Some researchers are investigating fewer than twenty markers in their DNA analysis (for example, Andersone et al., 2002; Grewal et al., 2003). Remember that using more loci means a better comparison, and even the "recreational" dog DNA tests use more than 100 loci.

The primary problem, however, is that of focus: no researchers are currently at work actually trying to make a test which can tell "wolf" from "dog," so the data they are collecting may only be marginally relevant to someone who just wants to know more about an unidentified animal. Most current research is aimed at examining the shape of the canid family tree through analysis of the DNA of various canids (Dr. Peter Savolainen comes to mind) or identifying genetic factors which could make dogs better "models" for research into human disease (Dr. Elaine Ostrander is a leader in this field).

Researchers like these are usually attempting to answer one small question about wolf or dog genetics; "How many thousands of years ago were wolves domesticated?" "What kind of variation occurs at this particular location on the DNA strand?" "What gene controls a certain physiological trait?" "How does variation at a particular locus change a dog's reaction to a virus?" (Parker, 2009; Spady, 2008; Wayne and Ostrander, 2007; Ostrander, 2004) These studies utilize DNA and may even compare the DNA of dogs and wolves to one another, but their limited scope—and focus on a topic *other* than, "Is animal X a wolf?"—generally make them, at this time, more of academic interest and less of relevance to a shelter worker trying to identify an animal.

No one has yet created a DNA database containing information about enough dogs to give an accurate picture of the genetics of the dog population across the United States. No research is currently underway to provide a good working picture of how percentage of wolf ancestry is related to expression of behaviors. No one is currently working on a reliable, scientifically accurate method to compare an unknown sample of DNA to the DNA of known animals in current pet populations to see if an unknown animal has wolf ancestry. And no one is currently evaluating the behavior of animals with reported recent wolf ancestry to see if there is any pattern relating that ancestry to non-pet-like behavior. Yes, you heard that right: *there is currently no working database which is designed to identify wolf ancestry in any animal based solely on DNA, and we have no scientifically confirmed relationship between percentage of wolf ancestry and displayed behavior.* So, even if we do send in a DNA test and prove that a given animal does not match any known breed or send DNA to a researcher to find that the animal has DNA markers which match those of a nearby population of wolves what does that information, alone, tell us about that animal's future behavior? *Nothing*.

The future

With further advances, DNA testing can only become more and more accurate, and likely someday the laboratories will have sufficient background information on both dogs and wolves to tell one from the other. However, this will take years of research, including, ideally, some research actually aimed at investigating the genetic nature of our canid companions, of whatever species. Until then, DNA testing, while useful in some limited contexts, is not of practical use for the rescue professional in predicting suitability as a pet in potential companion animals of unknown origin.

CHAPTER 8
Conclusions

The exciting world in which we live, where lawsuits lie around every corner, is not friendly to those wishing to take a risk on an unknown animal. What if we call it a dog, and it turns out to really be a wolf? We hope in this book that we have made a strong case to support our position: we still cannot easily, practically, and definitively tell dog from wolf in every instance. The paradigms of "dog" and "wolf" overlap to the point where some dogs either look or act, or both, like wolves—especially when one considers that common *expectations* of how wolves *should* act often color our assessments of unknown animals, leading us to think an animal is "acting like a wolf" when it is really just exhibiting some of the less commonly known aspects of normal dog behavior. We wish to assure the reader that, even after discarding the "wolf hybrid" label and giving all incoming animals the benefit of the doubt, a *good* behavior assessor is highly unlikely to accidentally slip a dangerous wild animal into someone's home.

8 — CONCLUSIONS

Another canid of indefinite origin. It looks "wolfy," but that alone does not make it unsuitable (or suitable!) as a pet. Photo courtesy of Monty Sloan.

While some people can and do successfully keep wolves as pets, most others would rather not once confronted with reality because most behavior displayed by wild wolves is generally considered inappropriate for display in a human home. Therefore, at most shelters, behavior assessors are looking for animals which display human-home-appropriate, "doggy" behaviors (which are *also* displayed by wolves, just not to the same extent). Wolves—real, actual wolves—which show up in a shelter or rescue facility are going to disqualify themselves, promptly and incontrovertibly, from being adoptable pets simply by virtue of displaying natural wolf behaviors, *whether they are labeled as wolves or not*. Whether one has had the animal identified as a wolf or a dog (or an elephant), the animal is still going to be displaying its natural behaviors, which will show up on the "radar" as inappropriate for most human homes. One is extremely unlikely to unintentionally let a wolf through a good behavioral analysis process. The likelihood of a wolf putting on its "dog's clothing" and sneaking under a good assessor's radar is very small. By contrast, the likelihood of a perfectly good dog acting or looking enough like a wolf to fool a casual observer and being denied an even initial behavioral assessment on the basis of that label is tragically large.

Our point here—our whole desire in writing this book—is that we want assessors to understand how sometimes dogs can give the wrong impression and be labeled as a "wolf hybrid" for incorrect reasons. We want assessors to give these "dubious" animals, which may have been labeled as "wolf hybrids" or "wolves" by people who may not have had all the facts at their disposal, the same fighting chance for a forever home that they give any other dog that enters their facility.

We have indeed had a long, strange trip through this book. We began by examining our preconceived notions of "wolf" and "dog" and saw how our mental pictures of wolves and hybrids may have been formed using, perhaps, not the most accurate of resources, simply because most of us do not have the kind of access to wolves and hybrids which is needed to form an accurate opinion. We have wandered the convoluted alleyways of evolution, to see that the wolf and the dog are so closely related that some scientists argue they are the same species. And hopefully, we have presented a case that this makes it not only possible, but indeed likely that the ranges of "dog" behavior and "wolf" behavior and physiology can (and do) overlap.

We then examined the genetics of hybridization between wolves and dogs and how genetics affects behavior and physiology. We watched chromosomes dance and followed the random assortment of genes which ensures that no two "50%" wolf hybrids will ever be exactly alike in their expression of "wolf" or "dog" behavior—not to mention "25%" hybrids, "99%" hybrids, dogs, wolves, etc. We examined the innumerable environmental factors which then alter the expression of genetically determined traits so that even a pure wolf may look like a dog, or vice versa. We have examined some common misconceptions about "wolf" and "dog" physiology and behavior and discovered that, in many cases, they are exactly the same thing.

How can evaluators, knowing how similar these animals are, knowing that they may even be considered the *same* animal, simply make a sweeping generalization based on one or two traits displayed in something as infinitely malleable as *looks* or as unbelievably variable as *behavior* to make a snap judgment about an animal's future?

Sometimes, the appellation of "wolf" or "wolf hybrid" is used as an excuse. When an animal clearly is not able to be placed, it is convenient to say, "Well, it's a wolf or a hybrid, it shouldn't be in someone's home." It saves time and trouble and nobody has to assess the animal or pay to keep it until it can be rehabilitated or further assessed. It just gets euthanized and we move on to more "obvious" animals. This harms the name of the dog's wild ancestors—maintaining this false association between bad behavior and recent wolf ancestry. *Perfectly ordinary dogs*, through bad socialization, unfortunate breeding, or abuse—or even sometimes because that's just *how dogs act*—sometimes behave like wolves. One does not need to invoke or further besmirch the oft-abused name of "wolf" in order to remove unsuitable animals from an adoption pool. The practice of calling anything with agouti fur or yellow eyes a "wolf" causes bad data in surveys because animals are being reported incorrectly, leading to misperceptions about how many wolves or hybrids are really in captivity. This leads to further bad feeling towards wolves who do not need any more bad feeling aimed at them, creates more misunderstandings about wolf (and dog) behavior, and causes perfectly good dogs to be euthanized for crimes they only *look* like they *might* commit.

8 — CONCLUSIONS

A wolf—but not a vicious, intractable, unpredictable, or uncontrollable animal. Photo courtesy of Monty Sloan.

Any animal that displays behaviors suitable for rescue, rehabilitation, and possibly being placed in a new home, deserves nothing less than the opportunity to have that happen, regardless of what label it may arbitrarily bear.

Appendix A
A Brief Mention of Another Suspicious Species

For simplicity's sake, we have almost entirely neglected in this book the (debatable) influence upon both wolves and dogs of coyotes *(Canis latrans)*, which exhibit their own distinct physical and behavioral characteristics, and which can and do interbreed with both dogs (Coppinger, 2009; Lauzon and Schitoskey, 1981; Fox 1978; Mahan and Gipson, 1976; Mengel, 1971) and wolves (Coppinger, 2009; Way, 2008; Mech, 1970).

The occurrence of coyotes interbreeding with red wolves *(Canis rufus)* has been reasonably well documented (Way, 2008) and is currently a point of contention where the preservation of red wolf populations is concerned. After all, if the population of red wolves in an area contains some individuals which are wolf/coyote hybrids, how does one preserve the red wolf species? How does one identify those individuals? How does one prevent them from reproducing and continuing the hybridization? What percentage of "coyote" genes in an animal constitutes a "hybrid" versus an animal which is naturally related to coyotes? The interbreeding of coyotes with dogs appears to have the same simple, straightforward story as the interbreeding of wolves with dogs (i.e., it is an equally convoluted nightmare).

A coyote. Photo courtesy of Monty Sloan.

Little scientific research (the most notable performed by Michael Fox in the mid 1970s) has been done on coyote/dog hybrids and most references tend to the anecdotal. Although everyone, especially in rural areas, seems to know someone who had a coydog, or shot a coydog, or had his or her pet attacked by a coydog, coyotes and dogs are prevented from routinely interbreeding by the same circumstances which generally prevent dogs and wolves from mixing—primarily social incompatibility (the two species do not speak the same canid "language") and territoriality on the part of both species (coyotes would in general drive a dog away as an intruder rather than attempting to court it). This is not to say that naturally-bred coydogs do not occur but that, like wolf hybrids, they are likely to be much more rare than public opinion would have one believe.

In captivity, of course, it is reasonably easy to get a coyote and a dog to reproduce, but coyotes can pose husbandry problems just as difficult as those posed by captive wolves, and people attempting to keep them generally find that they are just as troublesome to keep as any other wild creature. There are breeders out there deliberately producing coydogs for private sale, again, just as with wolves. However, it is (relatively) difficult to obtain and keep a wild coyote to breeding age and breeding stock animals in these operations are not always real coyotes or coyote x dog hybrids. Besides, unusually colored dog mixes sell better as "coydogs" than as "mutts!"

"Coydog" seems to be less of a real, commonly occurring hybridization between two species than it is vernacular shorthand for "it looks like a wolf, but it's too small to be a wolf hybrid." The animal is "clearly" not a wolf hybrid since it is so small, but it reminds the viewer either behaviorally or physiologically of a wolf or wild animal, so it "must be" a coyote cross, since coyotes are often considered to be "just" smaller versions of the wolf. Thus, if presented with a "coyote cross" or a "coydog," it may be worth one's while to, as with a "wolf hybrid," give the animal the same kind of benefit of the doubt before declaring it unplaceable. Small dogs can resemble wolves just as much as larger dogs. All dogs are descended from wolves—not just the large breeds.

A New Guinea Singing Dog. Photo by Jessica Addams.

There are two smaller breeds of dog which can confound the "coydog" label: the New Guinea Singing Dog and the Dingo. Both breeds are (arguably) descended from domesticated dogs which escaped (or were released) into the wild and founded wild (technically *feral*) populations. For the same reasons that wolves do (powerful natural selection for intelligence, prey drive, and territoriality), these animals can display very wolflike behavior despite being shaped very much like dogs. Just like wolves, the Singing Dog and the Dingo can be socialized, tamed, kept in captivity, and will interbreed with dogs. Occasionally, these animals, and/or their "hybrids" (real and imagined), will be encountered, although these seem to be much more rare than captive wolves and wolf hybrids.

Practically, all these unique animals can be handled with the same tools one uses to work with wolves or wolf hybrids. The same rules for the creation of hybrids, the identification of parent animals, the zebra effect, and the distribution of variation of looks and behavior in offspring of any litters apply to any animals presented as "coydogs," "Dingoes," "Singing Dogs," or their "hybrids."

Pop quiz: what would you do with an animal presented as *half-fox*?

Appendix B
Facility Contact Information

A good start acquiring the kind of background required to quickly and accurately identify wolves, hybrids, and dogs is to contact facilities working with wolves. Many of these facilities offer classes or seminars especially for people who wish to learn more about these animals. Wolf Park, for example, offers several multi-day seminars per year, including wolf hybrid seminars. The International Wolf Center also offers seminars, with a focus more on wild wolves and field research. For those seeking a more in-depth experience, facilities may also offer paid or unpaid internships, and we have yet to encounter an animal facility which was not interested in volunteers. These resources are up-to-date at the time of this book's publication. However, addresses and phone numbers do change.

Rescues
Animal Ark (www.animalark.org)
P. O. Box 60075
Reno, NV 89506-0001
1-775-970-3111

Mission: Wolf (www.missionwolf.com)
P. O. Box 1211
Westcliffe, CO 81252

Where Wolves Rescue
(www.wolfcountry.com/Where_Wolves_Rescue/)
30040 N 167th Ave
Surprise, AZ 85387
623-546-9653

Wild Spirit Wolf Sanctuary
(www.wildspiritwolfsanctuary.org)
HC 61 Box 28
Ramah, NM 87321
505-775-3304

W. O. L. F. (www.wolfsanctuary.net)
P. O. Box 1544
La Porte, CO 80535

Wolf facilities (U. S.)

International Wolf Center (www.wolf.org)
1396 Highway 169
Ely, MN 55731-8129
218-365-4695

Wolf Haven (www.wolfhaven.org)
3111 Offut Lake Rd.
SE Tenino, WA 98589
800-448-9653

Wolf Hollow (www.wolfhollowipswich.org)
114 Essex Rd.
Ipswich, MA 01938
978-356-0216

Wolf Park (www.wolfpark.org)
4004 E 800 N
Battle Ground, IN 47920
765-567-2265

Wolf Song of Alaska (www.wolfsongalaska.org)
P. O. Box 770950
Eagle River, AK 99577-0950
907-622-9653

Wolf Timbers (www.wolftimbers.org)
P. O. Box 107
Bolivar, OH 44612
330-874-7022

Wolf facilities (other countries)

Anglian Wolf Society (www.anglianwolf.com)
P. O. Box 1273
Wootton, England MK43 9WU
+44 0 844 414 2120

UK Wolf Conservation Trust (www.ukwolf.org)
UK Wolf Centre
ButlersFarm
Beenham
Reading
Berkshire, England
RG7 5NT
+44 0 118 971 3330

Wolf Science Center (www.wolfscience.at/english)Located in the Game Park Ernstbrunn
Dörfles, 2115 Ernstbrunn
Austria
info@wolfscience.at

Educational groups
Wild Sentry (www.wildsentry.org)
The Northern Rockies Ambassador Wolf Program INC.
P. O. Box 172
Hamilton, MT 59840

National Wildlife Federation (www.nwf.org)
11100 Wildlife Center Dr.
Reston, VA 20190
800-822-9919

Defenders of Wildlife (www.defenders.org)
1130 17th St. NW
Washington, D.C. 20036
800-385-9712

Online resources
The Wolf Dunn (inetdesign.com/wolfdunn)
Ralph Maughan's Wildlife Reports
(www.forwolves.org/ralph)
Yellowstone National Park's Wolf Information Page
(http://www.yellowstone-natl-park.com/wolf. htm)

Again, if your facility or website of choice does not appear here, that only means the authors have no firsthand knowledge of it. These places are not the only ones which have good working knowledge of wolves; they are just some of the ones we know best.

Recommended Reading

For those interested in a more complete picture of the wolf, the authors recommend the following books (among others too numerous to mention here):

- *The Wolf: The Ecology and Behavior of an Endangered Species,* by L. David Mech
- *Wolves: Behavior, Ecology, and Conservation,* edited by L. David Mech and Luigi Boitani
- *The Arctic Wolf: Ten Years With the Pack,* by L. David Mech
- *The Wolves of Yellowstone,* by Douglas W. Smith
- *The Wolves of Mount McKinley,* by Adolph Murie
- *Behaviour of Wolves, Dogs, and Related Canids,* by Michael W. Fox

Further information on red and Mexican gray wolves may be found here:

- U.S. Fish and Wildlife Service Mexican Gray Wolf Project (www.fws.gov/southwest/es/mexicanwolf/)
- The Red Wolf Coalition (www.redwolves.com)

For those interested in dog physiology and behavior:

- *The Domestic Dog: Its Evolution, Behaviour, and Interactions with People,* by James Serpell
- *The Dog's Mind,* by Bruce Fogle
- *Dogs: A New Understanding of Canine Origin, Behavior, and Evolution,* by Raymond and Lorna Coppinger

- *The Truth About Dogs: An Inquiry into the Ancestry, Social Conventions, Mental Habits, and Moral Fiber of Canis familiaris,* by Stephen Budiansky
- *Canine Behavior: A Photo Illustrated Handbook,* by Barbara Handelman
- *The Behavioural Biology of Dogs,* by P. Jensen
- *Dog Behaviour, Evolution, and Cognition,* by Ádám Miklósi
- *Genetics and the Social Behavior of the Dog,* by John Paul Scott and John L. Fuller

For further information on genetics, evolution, and domestication:
- By Lyudmila Trut: "Early Canid Domestication: The Farm Fox Experiment." *American Scientist* 87:160-169, 1999
- *The Cartoon Guide to Genetics,* by Larry Gonick
- *The Origin of Species,* by Charles Darwin
- *The Dog and Its Genome,* edited by Elaine Ostrander, Urs Giger, and Kerstin Lindblad-Toh
- *Dogs: A New Understanding of Canine Origin, Behavior, and Evolution,* by Raymond and Lorna Coppinger
- *A Natural History of Domesticated Mammals,* by Juliet Clutton-Brock
- *Domestication,* by Clive Roots
- *The Dog: Its Domestication and Behavior,* by Michael W. Fox
- *The Covenant of the Wild: Why Animals Chose Domestication,* by Stephen Budiansky

For information on wolf x dog hybrids:
- *Wolfdogs A-Z,* by Nicole Wilde
- *Living with Wolfdogs,* by Nicole Wilde
- *Above Reproach: A Guide for Wolf Hybrid Owners,* by Dorothy Prendergast
- *Wolf Hybrid,* by Dorothy Prendergast

Bibliography

Aiello, L. C. "Brains and guts in human evolution: the expensive tissue hypothesis." *Brazilian Journal of Genetics* 20(1):141-148, 1997.

Aldhous, P. "Handsome wolves stole dogs' black coat." *The New Scientist* 199(2675): 12, 2008.

Altreuther, P. "Safety and tolerance of enrofloxacin in dogs and cats." *Proceedings, 1st Int. Symposium on Baytril:* 15-19, 1992.

American Veterinary Medical Association. *Veterinary Biologics.* November 2008.

Andersone, Z, V. Lucchini, E. Randi, and J. Ozolins. "Hybridisation between wolves and dogs in Latvia as documented using mitochondrial and microsatellite DNA markers." *Mammalian Biology* 67(2):79-90, 2002.

Arnold, M. L. *Natural Hybridization and Evolution.* Oxford University Press, 1997.

Baker, B. "Mutts Decoded: DNA tests sort out canine family history." *The Boston Globe*, August 2, 2008.

Baker, P. J., S. M. Funk, M. W. Bruford, and S. Harris. "Polygynandry in a red fox population: implications for the evolution of group living in canids?" *Behavioral Ecology* 15(5):766-778, 2004.

Bargh, J. A., M. Chen, and L. Burrows. "Automaticity of social behavior: Direct effects of trait construct and stereotype activation on action." *Journal of Personality and Social Psychology* 71:230-244, 1996.

Bargh, J. A., and T. L. Chartrand. "The unbearable automaticity of being." *American Psychologist* 54:462-479, 1999.

Beck, A. *The Ecology of Stray Dogs*. Purdue University Press, 2002.

Bell, G. *Selection: The Mechanism of Evolution*. Oxford University Press, 2009.

Belyaev, D. K. "Domestication of animals." *Science Journal* 5:47-52, 1969.

Bissonnette, T. H. "Sexual photoperiodicity." *The Quarterly Review of Biology* 11:371, 1936.

Blount, Z. D., C. Z. Borland, and R. E. Lenski. "Historical contingency and the evolution of a key innovation in an experimental population of *Escherichia coli*." *Proceedings of the National Academy of Sciences* 105(23):7899-7906, 2008.

Boitani, L. and P. Ciucci. "Comparative social ecology of feral dogs and wolves." *Ethology, Ecology and Evolution* 7:49-72, 1995.

Bousé, D. *Wildlife Films*. University of Pennsylvania Press, 2000.

Brown, B. *A Man Among Wolves / In My Dreams I'm A Wolf*. "20/20" web article, http://abcnews.go.com/2020/story?id=3015683andpage=1, April 10, 2007. Accessed 9/12/09.

Busch, R. H. *The Wolf Almanac, New and Revised: A Celebration of Wolves and their World*. Lyons Press, 2007.

Cafazzo, S., P. Valsecchi, C. Fantini, and E. Natoli. "Social dynamics of a group of free-ranging domestic dogs living in a suburban environment." *Journal of Veterinary Behavior* 4(2): 61, 2009.

Call, J., J. Bräuer, J. Kaminsky, and M. Tomasello. "Domestic dogs (*Canis familiaris*) are sensitive to the attentional state of humans." *Journal of Comparative Psychology* 117(3): 257-263, 2003.

Callaway, E. "Dog genome provides clues to breeds' personalities." *The New Scientist* 198(2662):17, 2008.

Carmichael, L. E., G. Szor, D. Berteaux, M. A. Giroux, C. Cameron, and C. Strobek. "Free love in the far north: plural breeding and polyandry of arctic foxes (*Alopex lagopus*) on Bylot Island, Nunavut." *Canadian Journal of Zoology* 85(3):338-343, 2007.

Ciucci, P., V. Lucchini, L. Boitani, and E. Randi. "Dewclaws in wolves as evidence of admixed ancestry with dogs." *Canadian Journal of Zoology* 81(12): 2077-2081, 2003.

Clarke, T. "Exploring breed diversity in behavior in the domestic dog (*Canis familiaris*)." *Journal of Veterinary Behavior* 4(2): 101-102, 2008.

Clutton-Brock, J. *A Natural History of Domesticated Mammals.* Cambridge University Press, 1987.

Coleman, J. *Vicious: Wolves and Men in America.* Yale University Press, 2006.

Cooper, J. J., C. Ashton, S. Bishop, R. West, D. S. Mills, and R. J. Young. "Clever hounds: social cognition in the domestic dog (*Canis familiaris*)." *Applied Animal Behaviour Science* 81(3): 229-244, 2003.

Coppinger, R., L. Spector, and L. Miller. "What, if anything, is a wolf?" In *The World of Wolves: New Perspectives on Ecology, Behaviour and Management*, edited by M. Musiani, L. Boitani and P. Paquet. University of Calgary Press, 2009.

Coppinger, R. P. "What, if anything, is a wolf?" After-dinner speech at Canid Biology and Conservation Conference, Oxford University, UK. 2001.

Coppinger, R. P. and L. Coppinger. *Dogs: A New Understanding of Canine Origin, Behavior, and Evolution.* University of Chicago Press, New York, 2001.

Coppinger, R. P. and L. Coppinger. "Differences in the behavior of dog breeds." In *Genetics and the Behavior of Domestic Animals*, edited by T. Grandin, Academic Press, 1998.

Coppinger, R. P., J. Glendinning, E. Torop, C. Matthay, and M. Sutherland. "Degree of behavioral neoteny differentiates canid polymorphs." *Ethology* 75:89-108, 1987.

Coppinger, R. P. and R. Schneider. "The evolution of working dog behavior." In *The Domestic Dog: Its Evolution, Behaviour, and Interactions with People*, edited by J. Serpell, Cambridge University Press, 1995.

Crockford, S. J. *Dogs Through Time: An Archaeological Perspective.* Archaeopress, 2000.

Darwin, C. *On the Origin of Species by Means of Natural Selection.* Murray, London, 1859.

Derr, M. "Pack of Lies." *New York Times*, August 31, 2006.

Duman, E. *Differentiating Great Lakes Area Native Wild Wolves from Dogs and Wolf Dog Hybrids.* Earth Voices, 2001.

Evans, E. I. "The transport of spermatozoa in the dog." *American Journal of Physiology* 105:287-293, 1933.

Fatjó, J., D. Feddersen-Petersen, J. L. Ruiz de la Torre, M. Amat, M. Mets, B. Braus, and X. Manteca. "Ambivalent signals during agonistic interactions in a captive wolf pack." *Applied Animal Behaviour Science* 105(4): 274-283, 2007.

Forbes, S. H., and D. Boyd. "Genetic Variation of Naturally Colonizing Wolves in the Central Rocky Mountains." *Conservation Biology* 10(4):1082–1090, 1996.

Fox, M. W. *The Dog: Its Domestication and Behavior.* Garland STPM Press, 1978. Also available as an E-Book from Dogwise.com.

Fox, M. W. *The Wild Canids: Their Systematics, Behavioral Ecology and Evolution.* 1975; reprinted by Dogwise Press, 2009. Also available as an E-Book from Dogwise.com.

Fox, M. W. "Effects of domestication on prey catching and killing in beagles, coyotes, and F_2 hybrids." *Applied Animal Ethology* 2(2): 123-140, 1976.

Fox, M. W. "Behavior genetics of F_1 and F_2 coyote-dog hybrids." *Applied Animal Ethology* 1(2): 185-195, 1975.

Fox, M. W. "Social dynamics of three captive wolf packs." *Behaviour* 47(3-4): 290-301, 1973.

Fox, M. W. "Socio-ecological implications of individual differences in wolf litters: a developmental and evolutionary perspective." *Behaviour* 41(3-4): 298-313, 1972.

Fox, M. W. "The anatomy of aggression and its ritualization in canidae: a developmental and comparative study." *Behaviour* 35(3-4): 242-258, 1969.

Frank, H. (editor). *Man and Wolf.* Dr W. Junk Publishers, 1987.

Frank, H. and M. G. Frank. "On the effects of domestication on canine social development and behavior." *Applied Animal Ethology* 8(6): 507-525, 1982.

Fuller, J. L. "Photoperiodic control of the estrus in the Basenji." *Journal of Heredity* 47:179-80, 1956.

Gipson, P. S., W. B. Ballard, and R. M. Nowak. "Famous North American wolves and the credibility of early wildlife literature." *Wildlife Society Bulletin* 26(4): 808-816, 1998.

Glenn, J. L. W., Civitello, D. J. and S. L. Lance. "Multiple paternity and kinship in the gray fox (*Urocyon cinereoargenteus*)." *Mammalian Biology* 74(5):394-402, 2009.

Goodwin, D., Bradshaw, J. W. S. and Wickens, S. M. "Paedomorphosis affects agonistic visual signals of domestic dogs." *Animal Behavior* 53:297-304, 1997.

Grant, B. S. "Allelic melanism in American and British peppered moths." *Journal of Heredity* 95(2):97-102, 2004.

Grewal, S. K., P. J. Wilson, T. K. Kung, K. Shami, M. T. Theberge, J. B. Theberge, and B. N. White. "A genetic assessment of the eastern wolf (*Canis lycaon*) in Algonquin Provincial Park." *Journal of Mammalogy* 85(4): 625-632, 2004.

Haber, G. C. "The social structure and behavior of an Alaskan wolf population." M. A. Thesis, Northern Michigan University, Marquette, 1968.

Haber, G. C. "Socio-ecological dynamics of wolves and prey in a sub-arctic ecosystem." Ph. D. thesis, University of British Columbia, Vancouver, 1977.

Hall, E. R. "Cranial characters of a dog-coyote hybrid." *American Midland Naturalist* 29(2):371-374, 1943.

Hampton, B. *The Great American Wolf.* Macmillan, 1997.

Hemmer, H. *Domestication: The Decline of Environmental Appreciation.* (N. Beckhaus, trans.) Cambridge University Press, 2005.

Hope, J. "Wolves and wolf hybrids as pets are big business—but a bad idea." *Smithsonian Magazine*, June 1994.

Hu, Q., Q. Yang, O. Yamato, M. Yamasaki, Y. Maede, and T. Yoshihara. "Isolation and identification of organosulfur compounds oxidizing canine erythrocytes from garlic (*Allium Sativum*)." *Journal of Agricultural Food Chemistry* 50(5):1059-1062, 2002.

Iljin, N. A. "Wolf-dog Genetics." *Journal of Genetics* 42(3): 391– 427, 1941.

Jensen, P. *The Behavioural Biology of Dogs.* CABI Publishing, 2007.

Jochle, W. and A. C. Andersen. "The estrous cycle in the dog: a review." *Theriogenology* 7(3):113-140, 1977.

Johannes, J. E. "The Basenji annual estrus: controlled by short-day photoperiod." *The Basenji* 39(5):12-13, 2003.

Kahn, C. M. *Merck Veterinary Manual*, 9th Ed. Merck and Co, Inc., Whitehouse Station, NJ, 2008.

Karlsson, J. and M. Sjöström. "Human attitudes towards wolves, a matter of distance." *Biological Conservation* 137(4): 610-616, 2007.

Kramek, B. J. "The Hybrids Howl: Legislators Listen—These Animals Aren't Crying Wolf." *Rutgers Law Journal* 23, 1992.

Klaaren, K. J., S. D. Hodges, and T. D. Wilson. "Expectation whirls me round: The role of affective expectations in subjective experience and decision-making." *Social Cognition* 12(2): 77-101, 1994.

Klausz, B., A. Kis, E. Persa, and M. Gácsi. "Human-directed aggression in shelter dogs: how to test for better prediction of outcomes." *Journal of Veterinary Behavior* 4(2): 78, 2009.

Kolenosky, G. B. "Hybridization between wolf and coyote." *Journal of Mammalogy* 52(2):416-449, 1971.

Koler-Matznick, J. "The origin of the dog revisited." *Anthrozoos* 15(2): 98-118, 2002.

Kukekova, A., G. Acland, I. N. Oskina, A. V. Kharlamova, L. N. Trut, K. Chase, K. Lark, H. N. Erb, and G. D. Aguirre. "The genetics of domesticated behavior in canids: What can dogs and silver foxes tell us about each other?" *The Dog and its Genome*, Ostrander, E. A., Giger, U., Lindblad-Toh, K., ed., Cold Spring Harbor Laboratory Press, 2006.

Kyle, C. J., A. R. Johnson, B. R. Patterson, P. J. Wilson, K. Shami, S. K. Grewal, and B. N. White. "Genetic nature of eastern wolves: Past, present, and future." *Conservation Genetics* 7(2): 273-287, 2006.

Kyle, C. J., A. R. Johnson, B. R. Patterson, P. J. Wilson, and B. N. White. "The conspecific nature of eastern and red wolves: conservation and management implications." *Conservation Genetics* 9(3): 699-701, 2008.

Laikre L., N. Ryman, E. A. Thompson. "Hereditary Blindness in a Captive Wolf (*Canis lupus*) Population: Frequency Reduction of a Deleterious Allele in Relation to Gene Conservation." *Conservation Biology* 7(3):592–601, 1993.

Laikre, L., H. Tegelstrom, and H. P. Gelter. "DNA fingerprints of captive wolves (*Canis lupus*)." *Hereditas* 117:293-296, 1992.

Laikre, L. and N. Ryman. "Inbreeding Depression in a Captive Wolf (*Canis lupus*) Population." *Conservation Biology* 5:33–40, 1991.

Lange, K. "Wolf to woof: the evolution of dogs." *National Geographic* 201:2-11, 2002.

Lauzon, S. and F. Schitoskey, Jr. "Taxonomic status of coyotes from western South Dakota." *Proceedings of the South Dakota Academy of Sciences* 60:123-134, 1981.

Lee, L. *National Geographic throws Shaun Ellis to the wolves.* McClatchy-Tribune News Service, April 3, 2006.

Lehman, N., A. Eisenhawer, K. Hansen, D. L. Mech, R. O. Peterson, P. J. P. Grogan, and R. K. WayneS. "Introgression of coyote mitochondrial DNA into sympatric North American gray wolf populations." *Evolution* 45:104-119, 1991.

Lockwood, R. "Dominance in wolves—useful construct or bad habit." In *Symposium on the Behavior and Ecology of Wolves*, edited by E. Klinghammer. Garland STPM Press, 1979.

Lopez, B. *Of Wolves and Men.* Scribner, 1979.

Maargaard, L., and J. Graugaard. "Female Arctic wolf, *Canis lupus arctos*, mating with domestic dogs, *Canis familiaris*, in northeast Greenland." *Canadian Field-Naturalist* 108:374-375, 1994.

MacDonald, K. B. and B. E. Ginsburg. "Induction of normal prepubertal behavior in wolves with restricted rearing." *Behavioral and Neural Biology* 33(2): 133-162, 1981.

Mahan, B. R., and P. S. Gipson. "Osteoarthrosis in a coyote x dog hybrid from Nebraska." *Journal of Wildlife Diseases* 14:395-398, 1976.

McNamee, T. *The Return of the Wolf to Yellowstone.* Holt Paperbacks, 1998.

Mech, L. D. *The Wolf: The Ecology and Behavior of an Endangered Species.* Doubleday Publishing Co., 1970.

Mech, L. D. "Spacing and possible mechanisms of population regulation in wolves." *American Zoologist* 4:642, 1972.

Mech, L. D. "Population trend and winter deer consumption in a Minnesota wolf pack." In *Proceedings of the 1975 predator symposium*, Montana Forest and Conservation Experiment Station, edited by R. L. Phillips and C. Jonkel, pp 55-83, 1977.

Mech, L. D. *The Way of the Wolf.* Voyageur Press, 1993.

Mech, L. D., L. G. Adams, T. J. Meier, J. W. Burch, and B. W. Dale. *The Wolves of Denali.* University of Minnesota Press, 1998.

Mech, L. D. "Alpha status, dominance, and division of labor in wolf packs." *Canadian Journal of Zoology* 77:1196-1203, 1999.

Mech, L. D. and L. Boitani. *Wolves: Behavior, Ecology and Conservation.* University of Chicago Press, 2003.

Mengel, R. M. "A study of dog-coyote hybrids and implications concerning hybridization in *Canis*." *Journal of Mammalogy* 52(2):316-336, 1971.

Miklósi, A. *Dog Behaviour, Evolution, and Cognition.* Oxford University Press, 2007.

Miller, L. and S. Zawistowski. *Shelter Medicine for Veterinarians and Staff.* Blackwell, 2004.

Mitman, G. *Reel Nature: America's Romance with Wildlife on Film.* University of Washington Press, 2009.

Morell, V. "The origin of dogs: running with the wolves." *Science* 276:1647-1648, 1997.

Morey, D. "Size, shape and development in the evolution of the domestic dog." *Journal of Archaeological Science* 19(2): 181-204, 1992.

Murie, A. *The Wolves of Mount McKinley*. University of Washington Press, 1985.

National Association of State Public Health Veterinarians, Inc. *Compendium of Animal Rabies Prevention and Control*, 2008.

Nobis, G. "Der älteste Haushund lebte vor 14,000 Jahren." *Umschau* 19:610, 1979.

NOVA. "Dogs and More Dogs." WGBH Educational Foundation, 2004.

Ostrander, E. A., U. Giger, and K. Lindblad-Toh. *The Dog and Its Genome*. Cold Spring Harbor Laboratory Press, 2006.

Ostrander, E. A. and K. Comstock. "The domestic dog genome." *Current Biology* 14:98-99, 2004.

Ostrander, E. A. and L. Kruglyak. "Unleashing the canine genome." *Genome Research* 10(9):1271-1274, 2000.

Pal, S. K. "Parental care in free-ranging dogs, *Canis familiaris*." *Applied Animal Behaviour Science* 90(1): 31-47, 2005.

Paquet, P. C. and L. N. Carbyn. "Gray Wolf: *Canis lupus* and Allies" In *Wild Mammals of North America: Biology, Management, and Conservation, 2nd Edition*, edited by George A. Feldhamer, et al. JHU Press, 2003.

Park, K., J. Kang, S. Park, J. Ha, and C. Park. "Linkage of the locus for canine dewclaw to chromosome 16." *Genomics* 83(2): 216, 2004.

Parker, H. and E. A. Ostrander. "Genes for dogs: More than a fashion statement." *Journal of Veterinary Behavior* 4(2):70, 2008.

Parker, H. G., L. V. Kim, N. B. Sutter, S. Carlson, T. D. Lorentzen, T. B. Malek, G. S. Johnson, H. B. DeFrance, E. A. Ostrander and L. Kruglyak. "Genetic structure of the purebred domestic dog." *Science* 304:1093-1095. 2004.

Peterson, E. K. "Prolactin and seasonal reproduction in wolves." Dissertation, University of Minnesota, 1984.

Pierantoni, L. and M. Verga. "Behavioral consequences of premature maternal separation and lack of stimulation during the socialization period in dogs." *Journal of Veterinary Behavior* 2(3): 84-85, 2007.

Phemister, R. D., P. A. Hoist, J. S. Spano, and M. L. Hopwood. "Time of ovulation in the beagle bitch." *Biology of Reproduction*. 8:74-82, 1973.

Pilgrim, K. L., D. K. Boyd, and S. H. Forbes. "Testing for wolf-coyote hybridization in the Rocky Mountains using mitochondrial DNA." *Journal of Wildlife Management* 62(2): 683-689, 1998.

Prendergast, D. *The Wolf Hybrid.* Rudelhaus Enterprises, 1984.

Price, E. O. *Animal Domestication and Behaviour.* CABI Publishing, 2003.

Queller, D. and K. F. Goodnight. "Estimating relatedness using genetic markers." *Evolution* 43(2): 258-275, 1989.

Rabb, G. B., J. H. Woolpy, and B. E. Ginsburg. "Social relationships in a group of captive wolves." *American Zoologist* 7:305-311, 1967.

Räikkönen, J., J. A. Vucetich, R. O. Peterson, and M. P. Nelson. "Congenital bone deformities and the inbred wolves (*Canis lupus*) of Isle Royale." *Biological Conservation,* in press, 2009. doi:10. 1016/j. biocon. 2009. 01. 014

Räikkönen, J., A. Bignert, P. Mortensen, and B. Fernholm. "Congenital defects in a highly inbred wild wolf population (*Canis lupus*)." *Mammalian Biology* 71(2): 65-73, 2006.

Raipurohit, K. S. "Child lifting: wolves in Hazaribagh, India." *AMBIO* 28(2):162, 1999.

Randall, D. A., J. P. Pollinger, R. K. Wayne, L. A. Tallents, P. J. Johnson, and D. W. Macdonald. "Inbreeding is reduced by female-biased dispersal and mating behavior in Ethiopian wolves." *Behavioral Ecology* 10:579-589, 2007.

Randi, E. "Detecting hybridization between wild species and their domesticated relatives." *Molecular Ecology* 17(1): 285-293, 2008.

Rodier, L. "Mixed messages: can DNA tests really reveal the origin of your mixed-breed dog?" *Whole Dog Journal* 12(6): 4-11, 2009.

Rogers, L. J. and G. Kaplan. *Spirit of the Wild Dog: The World of Wolves, Coyotes, Foxes, Jackals, and Dingoes.* Allen and Unqin, 2003.

Ruvinsky, A. *The Genetics of the Dog.* CABI Publishing, 2002.

Sablin, M. V. and G. A. Khlopachev. "The earliest Ice Age dogs: Evidence from Eliseevivhi I." *Current Anthropology* 43:795-799, 2002.

Schassburger, R. M. "The vocal repertoire of the wolf: structure, function and ontogeny." Doctoral dissertation, Cornell University, 1978.

Schenkel, R. "Expression studies of wolves." *Behavior* 1:81-129, 1947.

Schmutz, S. M., T. G. Berryere, J. L. Barta, K. D. Reddick, and J. K. Schmutz. "Agouti sequence polymorphisms in coyotes, wolves and dogs suggest hybridization." *Journal of Heredity* 98(4): 351-355, 2007.

Schwab, C. and L. Huber. "Obey or not obey? Dogs (*Canis familiaris*) behave differently in response to attentional states of their owners." *Journal of Comparative Psychology* 120(3): 169-175, 2006.

Seal, U. S., E. D. Plotka, L. D. Mech, and J. M. Packard. "Seasonal metabolic and reproductive cycles in wolves." In *Man and Wolf*, edited by H. Frank, Dr W Junk Publishers, 1987.

Seal, U. S., E. D. Plotka, J. M. Packard, and L. D. Mech. "Endocrine correlates of reproduction in the wolf. I. Serum progesterone, estradiol and LH during the estrous cycle." *Reproduction* 21:1057-1066, 1979.

Siino, B. S. "Wolf Hybrids." *Dog Fancy*, January 1990.

Sillero-Zuburi, C., D. Gottelli and D. W. Macdonald. "Male philopatry, extra-pack copulations and inbreeding avoidance in Ethiopian wolves (*Canis simensis*)." *Behavioral Ecology and Sociobiology* 38(5):331-340, 1996.

Sloan, M. "America's Other Controversial Canine, the Wolf Hybrid." From Wolf Park's web site, http://www.wolfpark.org/aboutwolfhybrids.shtml. Accessed 6/13/09.

Sloan, M. "Of Wolves, Wolf Hybrids, and Children." Distributed by Wolf Park, Battle Ground, IN, 47920.

Smith, D. W. *Decade of the Wolf: Returning the Wild to Yellowstone*. Lyons Press, 2006.

Spady, T. C. and E. A. Ostrander. "Canine genomics: mapping behavioral traits." *Journal of Veterinary Behavior* 3(4):189, 2008.

Spady, T. C. and E. A. Ostrander. "Canine behavioral genetics: pointing out the phenotypes and herding up the genes." *American Journal of Human Genetics* 82(1): 10-18, 2007.

Steinhart, P. *The Company of Wolves*. Vintage, 1996.

Steward, R. C. "Industrial and non-industrial melanism in the peppered moth *Biston betularia*(L)." *Ecological Entomology* 2:231-243, 1977.

Stockton, S. *The Daily Coyote: A Story of Love, Survival and Trust in the Wilds of Wyoming*. Simon and Schuster, 2008.

Tami, G. and A. Gallagher. "Description of the behaviour of domestic dog (*Canis familiaris*) by experienced and inexperienced people." *Applied Animal Behaviour Science* 120(3-4): 159-169, 2009.

Thomas, J. "Difficulty of Breed Identification." Excerpt from "What is BSL?" on *www.stopbsl.com*. Accessed 6/14/09.

Thurston, M. E. *The Lost History of the Canine Race: Our 15,000-Year Love Affair With Dogs.* Avon Books, 1997.

Trut, L. N. "Early canid domestication: the farm fox experiment." *American Scientist* 87:160-169, 1999.

Trut, L. N., I. Z. Plyusnina and I. N. Oskina. "An experiment on fox domestication and debatable issues of evolution of the dog." *Russian Journal of Genetics* 40(6):644-655, 2004.

Tsuda, K., Y. Kikkawa, H. Yonekawa, and Y. Tanabe. "Extensive interbreeding occurred among multiple matriarchal ancestors during the domestication of dogs: evidence from inter– and intraspecies polymorphisms in the D-loop region of mitochondrial DNA between dogs and wolves." *Genes and Genetic Systems* 72: 229-238, 1997.

Tucker, P. and B. Weide. "The romance of having a wolf of your very own." *International Wolf*, Fall 2003.

Tucker, P. and B. Weide. *Can You Turn A Wolf Into A Dog?* Published by Wild Sentry, Box 172, Hamilton, MT, 58940.

Udell, M. A. R., N. R. Dorey, and C. D. L. Wynne. "Wolves outperform dogs in following human social cues." *Animal Behaviour* 76(6): 1767-1773, 2008.

Vilà C., C. Walker, A-K Sundqvist, O. Flagstad, Z. Andersone, A. Casulli, I. Kojola, H. Valdmann, J. Halverson, and H. Ellegren. "Combined use of maternal, paternal and bi-parental genetic markers for the identification of wolf-dog hybrids." *Heredity* 90:17-24, 2003.

Vilà C., J. E. Maldonado, and R. K. Wayne. "Phylogenetic relationships, evolution, and genetic diversity of the domestic dog." *Journal of Heredity* 90:71-77, 1999.

Vilà C. and R. K. Wayne. "Hybridization between Wolves and Dogs." *Conservation Biology* 13(1):195–198, 1999.

Vilà, C., P. Savolainen, J. E. Maldonado, I. R. Amorim, J. E. Rice, R. L. Honeycutt, K. A. Crandall, J. Lundeberg, and R. K. Wayne. "Multiple and Ancient Origins of the Domestic Dog." *Science* 276:1687-1689, 1997.

Walker, D. and G. C. Frison. "Studies on Amerindian dogs, 3: Prehistoric wolf/dog hybrids from the northwest plains." *Journal of Archaeological Science* 92:125-172, 1982.

Walker, S. L. "Aspects of reproductive endocrinology in the red wolf (*Canis rufus*)." Dissertation, University of Guelph, 2000.

Watanabe, T., Y. Sasaki, and J. Nanez. "Perceptual learning without perception." *Nature* 413:844-848, 2001.

Way, J. G. "Eastern coyote: coyote, wolf, or hybrid?" *International Wolf* 18(3):7-10, 2008.

Way, J. G. "Coywolf: Uncovering the Genetic Secrets of the Eastern Coyote." *Nature Photographers Online Magazine*, December 2008: *www.naturephotographers.net/articles1208/jw1208-1.html*. Accessed 8/21/09.

Way, J. G., D-L M. Szumylo, and E. G. Strauss. "An ethogram developed on captive Eastern Coyotes, *Canis latrans*." *Canadian Field-Naturalist* 120(3):263-288.

Wayne, R. "Consequences of domestication: Morphological diversity of the dog." *The Genetics of the Dog*, Ruvinsky, A., Sampson, J., ed., CABI Publishing, 2001.

Wayne, R. "Molecular evolution of the dog family." *Trends in Genetics* 9(6): 218-224, 1993.

Wayne, R. and E. A. Ostrander. "Lessons learned from the dog genome." *Trends in Genetics* 23(11): 557-567, 2007.

Wayne, R. and E. A. Ostrander. "Origin, genetic diversity, and genome structure of the domestic dog." *BioEssays* 21:247-257, 1999.

Wickens, S. M. and J. W. S. Bradshaw. "Dominance relationships in groups of domestic dogs (*Canis familiaris*)." *Applied Animal Behaviour Science* 35(3): 291, 1993.

Willems, R. A. "The Wolf-Dog Hybrid—An Overview of a Controversial Animal." *AWIC Newsletter*, USDA, 1995.

Wilson, D. and D. M. Reeder. *Mammal Species of the World: A Taxonomic and Geographic Reference.* Second edition. Smithsonian Institution Press, Washington, D. C., 1993.

Wilson, E. O. *Sociobiology.* Harvard University Press, 1975.

Wolf Is At The Door, Inc. *Wolf-Dog Hybrids: the Good, the Bad, and the Ugly.* 2003. Via http://www.wolf-to-wolfdog.org/publications.htm. Accessed 8/30/09.

Yang, F., P. C. M. O'Brien, B. S. Milne, A. S. Graphodatsky, N. Solanky, V. Trifonov, W. Rens, D. Sargan and M. A. Ferguson-Smith. "A complete comparative chromosome map for the dog, red fox, and human and its integration with canine genetic maps." *Genomics* 62(2): 189-202, 1999.

Zawistowski, S. L. and P. J. Reid. "Deeming Dogs Dangerous by Breed in the U. S.: Fact or Politics?" *Viewpoint* discussion on *www.washingtonpost.com*. Accessed 6/13/09.

Zimen, E. "On the regulation of pack size in wolves." *Z. Tierpsychol.* 40:300-341, 1976.

Zimen, E. "A wolf pack sociogram." In *Wolves of the World*, edited by F. H. Harrington and P. C. Paquet. Noyes Publishers, 1982.

Zimen, E. "Ontogeny of approach and flight behavior towards humans in wolves, poodles and wolf-poodle hybrids." In *Man and Wolf*, edited by H. Frank, Dr. W. Junk Publishers, 1987.

About the Authors

"Jessica and Andrew both have extensive experience working with wolves and wolf dog hybrids. Having years of experience at Wolf Park and having traveled around the country visiting various facilities across the US, they have accrued extensive knowledge and experience on the handling, care, and identification of wolves, dogs, and wolf hybrids." ~ Monty Sloan, wolf behaviorist and photographer

Over the course of this book, we have spent much time detailing the caveats of several sources of information. It would not, then, be fair for the authors, two individuals who do not own wolf hybrids themselves (one owns a yellow Labrador, the other is owned by a German Shepherd) not to offer as background the experience that we *do* have with wolves and wolf hybrids.

Our primary wolf experience comes from nearly twenty years of collective work at Wolf Park, a non-profit education and research facility in Battle Ground, Indiana. Wolf Park was founded in 1972 by Dr. Erich Klinghammer and is the premier facility for the study of captive wolf behavior, husbandry, and socialization in the world. Park staff regularly teach seminars on these topics to keepers from other institutions, training them how to handle captive adult wolves as well as how to socialize and train young wolves to interact safely with humans. Their work concerning socialization and environmental enrichment has enhanced the husbandry routines of many facilities, and several other facilities have been founded based on their teachings. Both authors have been involved with Wolf Park for many years, starting as visitors, moving up to long-term internships, and eventually becoming full-time staff.

About the Authors

During our careers at Wolf Park, both authors regularly handled socialized wolves, foxes, and coyotes, as well as instructing others in the handling and training of same. Both authors have been "puppy parents," people who raise the Park's young pups from fourteen days to three months of age, helping to socialize them to humans—and, just as importantly, training humans to properly interact with the wolves. We have designed enclosures, created environmental enrichment items, administered medication, and worked on managing husbandry issues. We also lived with a low-content wolf hybrid for a few years, as tenants in its owner's home.

Since people visit the Park regularly with questions about wolves, hybrids, and dog behavior, the authors have seen many such animals over the years, and worked with a variety of people who "run with the wolves": from scared new owners who did not intend to end up with a wolf, to people who had rescued a wolf from an unsuitable home, to people who planned to open a wolf sanctuary, to people who just wanted to know why their Husky howled all the time. We wrote educational materials for these persons, helped them on the phone with solving behavior problems and generating training ideas and, when necessary, referred them to a properly vetted wolf rescue. In many cases, owners or rescues sent photos of unknown animals, asking for information about their heritage, and, from that unending series of queries, this book was born.

This is where a great deal of the information in this book originates—from our decades of collective experience at Wolf Park, watching the wolves, watching wolves at other facilities, working with the staff of those facilities, meeting people who owned wolves or hybrids, and even watching our own pets. Before we arrived at Wolf Park, the facility had been working with wolves for more than twenty-five years, and we learned immeasurable amounts from the Park staff as well.

Before writing this book, we visited a number of wolf rescues all across the United States, asking them about their animals, their stories, their attempts to educate people about wolves and hybrids, and what information they would want to impart to someone who was trying to identify an unknown animal. We also spoke with wolf breeders. We have seen wolves who look like dogs, dogs who look like wolves, and everything in between.

Besides our work with wolves, we have always been involved with animals and the study of animal behavior. Our degrees are in biology and wildlife science. We own and train our own dogs and other pets, and we read voraciously. Meanwhile, we are, of course, still learning. Part of why we love what we do is that we learn something new every day.

INDEX

A
Afghan Hounds, 26
aggressive behavior
    in dogs, 44
    environmental impacts on, 94–96
    rank order and, 33–34
    toward other canines, 132–133
    of wolves compared to dogs, 127
aging, effects of, 84, 92–93, 129
Aiello, L.C., 56
AKC (American Kennel Club), 74, 86, 146, 147
Alaskan Malamutes. See Malamutes
albinism, 77
Aldhous, P., 52
alleles, 66–68, 142–144
alpha wolves
    feeding behavior and, 6
    hunting and, 15
    rank orders, 32
American Kennel Club, 74, 86, 146, 147
American Staffordshire Terriers, 89–90. See also Pit Bulls
anatomical features. See physical characteristics
Anderson, A.C., 135
Andersone, Z., 148
Animal Welfare Information Center, 101
Auel, Jean M., 14

B
Baker, P.J., 88
Bargh, John, 100
barking, 58, 91, 122–123
Basenjis, 114, 123
Bassett Hounds, 115
Beagles, 27
behavioral characteristics of dogs
    compared to wolves, 90–98, 124–128
    drives for rank and territories, 46–47
    overview, 22–23, 43–44
    prey drive, 44–46
behavioral characteristics of wolves
    compared to dogs, 90–98, 122–128
    overview, 20–22, 28–29
    prey drive, 37–41
    social groups, 30–37
    territories, 41–43
Belyaev, Dmitry, 68–69
Bissonnette, T.H., 135
Blount, Z.D., 54
body language. See communication
Boitani, L., 18
books on wolves
    availability of, xii
    misinformation and, 12–16
    recommended reading, 161–162
Border Collies
    escape behavior and, 127
    eye color of, 111
    predatory behavior and, 45, 91
    spontaneous mutations and, 78
Born Free, 14
Borzois, 27, 45
Boxers, 61
Bradley, Janis, 89
Bradshaw, J.W.S., 46
brain size, 29
breed standards, 74
breeding cycles
    of dogs, 28
    evaluations for identification and, 129, 135–136
    multiple paternity and, 88
    of wolves, 24
Bull Terriers, 27, 90
Bulldogs, 27
Busch, R.H., 117

C
Cafazzo, S., 46
Call, J., 96
Canadian Eskimo Dogs, 87
captive wolves
    aggression and, 33–34

breeding programs and, 102–103
children and, 39–41
rank order and, 36
taming processes of, 60
Carbyn, L.N., 102
Carmichael, L.E., 88
Cartoon Guide to Genetics (Gonick), 141
Charles River Laboratories, 78
chest sizes, 105, 115–116
Chihuahuas, 22, 27, 59, 105, 126
children
    attacks on, 6
    books on wolves, 13
    evaluations for identification and, 131–132
    predatory behavior and, 39–41, 45
chromosomes, 65–66
Ciucci, P., 7, 106
claws, 115–116
Clutton-Brock, J., 58
coat patterns, 23, 108, 109–110, 117
Cockapoos, 88
Cocker Spaniels, 87
Coleman, J., 13
Collies, 27, 45, 78
communication
    among wolves, 31–36
    between wolves and men, 11
Coppinger, Lorna, 56, 85, 101
Coppinger, R.P., 52, 53, 56, 59, 61, 85, 87, 91, 101, 154
corticosteroids, 57
coyotes, 14, 154–157
Crockford, S.J., 135
Czechoslovakian Wolf Dog, 2, 3, 86–87, 118

D

Dachshunds, 117
"Daily Coyote", 14
Dances with Wolves, 12
defects, 80–81

deoxyribonucleic acid. See DNA (deoxyribonucleic acid)
destructiveness, 124
dewclaws, 106, 115–116
diet, 81–82, 94–95
digging, 127
Dingos, 156–157
diseases, 94
DNA (deoxyribonucleic acid)
    of dogs compared to wolves, 52–53
    explained, 63–71
    tests for, 99, 139, 140–149
Dobermans, 44, 78
documentaries about wolves, 10–12
Dog: Its Domestication and Behavior, The (Fox), 62
dog-oids, defined, 1–2
Dogs, A New Understanding of Canine Origin, Behavior and Evolution (Coppinger and Coppinger), 56
Dogs Bite, but Balloons and Slippers are More Dangerous (Bradley), 89
domestic stock, 6–7, 13
domestication
    compared to training, 59–60
    effects of, 60–62, 90
    evolutionary processes and, 50–59
dominance behavior, 12, 16, 30–36, 95
drugs, 94
Dutcher, Jim and Jamie, 16

E

ear sizes, 108, 109, 111
Earth's Children (Auel), 14
Ellis, Shaun, 15
endangered species, 26
Endangered Species Act, 102
environmental pressures
    effect on behavior of wolves, 28–29
    evolutionary processes and, 21–22, 54
    physical variations and, 84
    on wolves compared to dogs, 21–23
epilepsy, 94
estrous cycles, 24, 28, 88, 129, 135–136

evaluations for identification
   behavioral characteristics, 122–128
   importance of, 151–152
   intake information, 128–134
   overview, 99–104
   physical evaluations, 105–122
Evans, E. I., 88
evolution, defined, 53–57
expectations, evaluation of, 100–101
eyes, 23, 108, 109, 111

F

facial markings, 117–118
Fatjó, J., 148
feeding behavior. See also predatory behavior
   of alpha wolves, 6
   growling and, 11
   rank order and, 33
feral dogs, 101, 156
Fox, M.W., 44, 56, 58, 62, 74, 154, 155
Frank, H., 56, 59, 61
Frank, M.G., 56, 59, 61
Fuller, J.L., 135
fur coloring, 23, 108, 109–110, 117

G

gel electrophoresis, 142
genetics, 63–71, 152. See also DNA (deoxyribonucleic acid)
Genetics and the Social Behavior of the Dog (Scott and Fuller), 92
George, Jean Craighead, 13
German Shepherds
   eligibility as pets, 136–137
   line breeding and, 80
   physical characteristics of, 75–77, 111
   similarities to wolves, 87
   size of, 23, 26–27
gestation periods, 24, 28
Ginsburg, B.E., 148
Gipson, P.S., 13, 154
Glenn, J.L., 88
Gonick, Larry, 141

Goodwin, D., 61, 62
Greenland Dogs, 87
greeting behaviors, 123
Grewal, S.K., 148
Greyhounds, 27, 45, 117, 119
guarding behavior, 134

H

Haber, G.C., 32, 34
Halliburton Forest Wolf Centre, 80
Hampton, B., 13
head sizes, 105–107
Hope, J., 101
hormone imbalances, 94
Hounds, 44
howling, 91, 97, 126–127
Huber, L., 96
hunting behavior. See predatory behavior
Huskies. See Siberian Huskies

I

Iljin, N.A., 140
illness, 94
inbreeding, 79–80
information sources
   attaching labels and, 100–101
   based on experiences, 5–10, 16–17
   literature, 12–16
   problems with, xi–xii
   reliable sources, 17–19, 158–162
   visual media, 10–12
injuries, effects of, 84
intake information, 128–130
intelligence, 29, 134–135
interbreeding
   barriers to, 52
   with coyotes, 154
   DNA and, 63–71
Inuit dogs, 86
Isle Royale, 80

J

Japanese Chins, 27
Jochle, W., 135

Julie of the Wolves (George), 13
juvenile canines
  behaviors of, 61, 92–93
  physical characteristics of, 122

K
Kahn, Cynthia M., 93
Karlesson, J., 10
Kavika: Tales of a Timber Wolf, 14
Khlopachev, G.A., 55
Klaaren, K.J., 100
Klausz B., 96
Klinghammer, Erich, 59
Kukekova, A., 59
Kyle, C.J., 52, 148

L
labels, 100–101
Labradoodles, 88
Labrador Retrievers, 27, 68, 74, 111
Laikre, L., 80, 148
Lauzon, S., 154
leg lengths, 109, 114
Lehman, N., 52
Lhasa Apsos, 134
line breeding, 79–80
litter sizes, 24, 28
livestock, 6–7, 13
loci (of DNA), 141–146
Lockwood, R., 33
Lopez, Barry, xi

M
MacDonald, K.B., 148
Mahan, B.R., 154
Malamutes
  barking and, 122–123
  coats of, 117
  eligibility as pets, 137
  facial markings of, 118
  howling and, 126–127
  misinformation and, 17
  similarities to wolves, 26, 85–86, 90
  tails of, 23, 113
Mammal Species of the World (Smithsonian Institute), 52
markers (in DNA), 141, 147
Mars WisdomPanel MX Mixed Breed Analysis test, 147
Mastiffs, 105
McConnell, Patricia B., 74, 89
Mech, L.D., 18, 32, 38, 154
medications, 94
meiosis, 65–66
Mendel, Gregor, 68
Mengel, R.M., 154
Millan, Cesar, 16
misinformation about wolves. See information sources
mitochondria, 146
mixed breed dogs, 87–88, 144–147
Modoc, 14
movies about wolves, 10–12
multiple paternity, 88
Murie, A., 32
mutations, 77–78
myths about wolves. See information sources

N
neoteny, 61
neurological diseases, 94
neutering, 129
Never Cry Wolf (Mowat), 12
New Guinea Singing Dogs, 156–157
Newfoundlands, 27, 105
Nobis, G., 55
Norwegian Elkhounds, 87
noses, 109, 112
nutrition, 81–82, 94–95

O
Of Wolves and Men (Lopez), xi
omega wolves, 34–35

organelles, 146
Ostrander, E.A., 55
Ostrander, Elaine, 148
Other End of the Leash, The (McConnell), 74, 89

P

pack behavior
    dog training and, 16
    rank order and, 30–36
Paquet, P.C., 102
Park, K., 106
Parker, H., 148
paw sizes, 105, 117, 119
PCR (polymerase chain reaction), 142
pedigree method, 70–71
pedomorposis, 61
Penn and Teller's B.S., 11–12
Peterson, E.K., 135
Petit Basset Griffon Vendeens, 89
physical characteristics
    of dogs, 26–28
    variations in, 73–90
    of wolves, 23–26
Pierantoni, L., 95
Pilgrim, K.L., 52
Pit Bulls, 89–90, 146
play behavior, 33–34, 92–93
polymerase chain reaction (PCR), 142
Pomeranians, 27
Poodles, 26, 27
Pound Mouse, 78
precaudal glands, 115, 117
predatory behavior
    evaluations for identification and, 131–132
    prey drive in dogs, 44–46, 91
    prey drive in wolves, 37–41
public education programs, 17–18
pups. See also juvenile canines
    rank order and, 34
    rearing of, 31

R

Rabb, G.B., 33
rabies, 94
Räikkönen, J., 80
Raipurohit, K.S., 39
Randall, D.A., 88
Randi, E., 106
rank orders, 16, 30–36, 46–47, 95
reproductive maturity, 31, 37
resource guarding, 41–43, 46–47
Rottweilers, 44
Ryman, N., 80

S

Sablin, M.V., 55
Samoyeds, 87, 89
Sarloos Wolfhounds, 87
Savolainen, Peter, 148
scent marking, 42–43, 95
Schassburger, R.M., 122
Schenkel, R., 33, 34
Schitoskey, F., 154
Schneider, R., 56, 59, 61
Schwab, C., 96
Seal, U.S., 37
selective breeding
    breed standards and, 74–77
    dogs that resemble wolves and, 85–87
    domestication and, 57–59
    effects of behavior on dogs and, 22–23, 43–44, 46–47
    line breeding and, 79–80
seratonin, 69–70
Shar-Peis, 27
Shitz Tzus, 89
short tandem repeat (STR), 141
shyness, 125–126
Siberian Huskies
    barking and, 122
    eligibility as pets, 137
    misidentification of, 1
    physical characteristics of, 105, 111, 117–119

similarities to wolves, 26, 79, 85–86, 90
tails of, 23, 113
training behaviors and, 135
Siino, B.S., 90
Sillero-Zubiri, C., 88
sizes
    of dogs, 26–27, 109–110
    of wolves, 23
Sjöström, M., 10
skull morphology assessments, 140
Sloan, Marty, xi–xii
social behavior
    effects of age on, 92–93
    importance of, 95–96, 152
    pack behavior and, 30–37, 46–47
    toward humans, 133–134
    of wolves compared to dogs, 125–126
Spady, T.C., 148
spaying, 129
species
    defined, 50–51
    of wolves, 24–26
Spirit of the Wolf (Ellis), 15
spontaneous mutations, 77–78
sports, 97
Steward, R.C., 54
Stockton, Shreve, 14
stops, 120–121
STR (short tandem repeat), 141
Systema Naturae (Linnaeus), 50

T
tails, 23, 105–106, 109, 113
taming processes, 59–60
television, 10–12, 15–16
Terriers, 44
territories
    drive for, 41–43
    effects on behavior, 96
    marking behavior, 30
    rank orders and, 95
testing in rank order, 36
toys, 42

training behaviors, 123–124, 134–135
Trut, L.N., 57, 61
Tsuda, K., 52
Tucker, Pat, 29

U
Udell, M.A.R., 125
Unbearable Automaticity of Being, The (Bargh), 100
U.S. Pet Ownership and Demographics Sourcebook, 101

V
variable number tandem repeat (VNTR), 141
variations of wolves, 24–26
veterinary schools, 16
Vilà, C., 22, 52, 58, 148
VNTR (variable number tandem repeat), 141

W
Walker, S.L., 135
Watanabe, T., 10
Way, J.G., 154
Wayne, R., 52, 57, 61, 148
Wesley the Owl, 14
"What, if Anything, is a Wolf?" (Coppinger), 53
White Fang (London), 12
Wickens, S.M., 46
Wilde, Oscar, 20
Willems, R.A., 66, 68, 101
Wilson, E.O., 117
"Wolf Dunn," 18
wolf hybrids, defined, x
Wolf Park
    authors' experiences, 1
    educational efforts, 59, 101, 105, 131
    inbreeding and, 80
    reliable sources, 17–18
Wolfhounds, 87
Wolves (IMAX), 11
wolves, defined, x

Wolves at Our Door (Dutcher), 14, 16
Wolves: Behavior, Ecology and Conservation (Mech and Boitani), 18

X
Xoloitzcuintlis, 27

Y
Yorkshire Terriers, 26

Z
zebra effect, 97, 103
Zimen, E., 33, 74

Notes

Selected Titles From Dogwise Publishing
www.dogwise.com 1-800-776-2665

BEHAVIOR & TRAINING

Barking. The Sound of a Language. Turid Rugaas
Bringing Light to Shadow. A Dog Trainer's Diary. Pam Dennison
Canine Behavior. A Photo Illustrated Handbook. Barbara Handelman
Canine Body Language. A Photographic Guide to the Native Language of Dogs. Brenda Aloff
Chill Out Fido! How to Calm Your Dog. Nan Arthur
Do Over Dogs. Give Your Dog a Second Chance for a First Class Life. Pat Miller
Dogs are from Neptune. Jean Donaldson
Oh Behave! Dogs from Pavlov to Premack to Pinker. Jean Donaldson
On Talking Terms with Dogs. Calming Signals, 2nd edition. Turid Rugaas
Play With Your Dog. Pat Miller
Positive Perspectives. Love Your Dog, Train Your Dog. Pat Miller
Positive Perspectives 2. Know Your Dog, Train Your Dog. Pat Miller
Stress in Dogs. Martina Scholz & Clarissa von Reinhardt
Tales of Two Species. Essays on Loving and Living With Dogs. Patricia McConnell
When Pigs Fly. Train Your Impossible Dog. Jane Killion

HEALTH & ANATOMY, SHOWING

An Eye for a Dog. Illustrated Guide to Judging Purebred Dogs. Robert Cole
Another Piece of the Puzzle. Pat Hastings
Canine Massage. A Complete Reference Manual. Jean-Pierre Hourdebaigt
The Canine Thyroid Epidemic. W. Jean Dodds and Diana Laverdure
Dog Show Judging. The Good, the Bad, and the Ugly. Chris Walkowicz
The Healthy Way to Stretch Your Dog. A Physical Therapy Approach. Sasha Foster and Ashley Foster
It's a Dog Not a Toaster. Finding Your Fun in Competitive Obedience. Diana Kerew
Tricks of the Trade. From Best of Intentions to Best in Show, Rev. Ed. Pat Hastings
Work Wonders. Feed Your Dog Raw Meaty Bones. Tom Lonsdale

Dogwise.com is your complete source for dog books on the web! 2,000+ titles, fast shipping, and excellent customer service.

www.ingramcontent.com/pod-product-compliance
Lightning Source LLC
Chambersburg PA
CBHW080542170426
43195CB00016B/2653